# *the* girl factory

# *the* girl factory

## A MEMOIR

### KAREN DIETRICH

Guilford, Connecticut
*An imprint of Globe Pequot Press*

skirt!® is an attitude . . . spirited, independent, outspoken, serious, playful and irreverent, sometimes controversial, always passionate.

Project editor: Meredith Dias
Layout: Maggie Peterson

Library of Congress Cataloging-in-Publication Data is available on file.

ISBN 978-0-7627-9181-1

Printed in the United States of America

10 9 8 7 6 5 4 3 2 1

*For my father, who told me to write books.*

# Contents

# Contents

# PART ONE

*I imagine a place where girls are made. Some roll off the assembly line shiny and wet, wheat-colored hair sewn into their beautiful heads like dolls. Other girls are assembled from spare parts, pieces the glossy girls refuse—a leg here, an elbow there—our maker scavenging for anything to use. Building girls like me is lonely work, no reward for the journeyman, no bright fame. Inside the girl factory, it is dark as midnight, the workers toiling away, unable to see their hands. There are so many mistakes to be made, which is why I know there must be girls like me out there somewhere. I'm the glass thrown onto the cullet belt with a smash. I break into a hundred sharp pieces. The belt leads underground, where girls like me are melted, poured into molds so the maker can try again, try to get it right this time. But I keep coming out flawed—cold crizz, chip finish, bird swing. I look whole, yet crumble with a touch. I'm thrown back to the cullet, back to the melting pot, where I keep trying to come out right.*

# CHAPTER 1

# Bread and Butter

When I sit perfectly still, the stars seem to dim then brighten like a pulse, a metronome of breathing. My mother is next to me in the grass. I am eight years old and she is telling me about shooting stars. She says if you see one, it means someone you love is about to die. My eyes scan the stars, which are splattered in clumps, as if someone has thrown handfuls of light against the dark. I hope everything stays put for now.

My mother knows a lot about the sky. She teaches me things: where to find the Big and Little Dippers, how to spot Orion's belt on a clear night, how to track the phases of the moon. There are rhymes to help me remember certain things. *Red sky at night, sailors delight.* I spend hours in darkness stretched out in the yard, looking up. My mother says there's a star for every person alive in the world. That's why you see a falling star when someone dies. The sky doesn't need that star anymore, so the sky sends the star to you.

"Are you supposed to catch it?" I ask.

"Why sure," she tells me, "if you can run fast enough." She pulls herself up, gently brushing a few damp blades of grass from her jeans. "If you can find the spot where the star fell to Earth, then that person you love won't die after all." She disappears up the back porch steps and into the house, its windows blinking through sheer curtains that sway in the evening breeze.

As long as I can remember, my mother has been teaching me what my father calls *Mother's ways*. I know to knock on wood when I think about good luck, like never breaking a bone in my body. If I don't, the spirits of bad luck will scold me for boasting, and curse me with a broken ankle or arm, their way of reminding me of my place in the world. If you can't find wood, knocking on your head is the next best thing. Knocking on glass or plastic is actually worse than not knocking at all. There are things you should never do, like break a mirror or use your oven on Sunday or let a bird fly into your house. Then there are things you must do: throw salt over your shoulder after you spill some, shake an empty purse at the full moon, say "bread and butter" if you're walking down the street with a friend and something comes between the two of you, like a telephone pole or another person.

I have a recurring dream. In it, I am walking alone on a slick black road. There are no houses, no streetlights, no trees, nothing to distract my view of the sky, which is inky blue. It has a texture. If I reach up to touch it, it will feel like corduroy, millions of soft raised rows, perfectly spaced, like cornrows. There is only one star in the sky, and even though no one in the dream tells me this, I know it is because I am the last person on Earth.

All of my mother's family is dead, except for one brother, Jack-Rogers, who lives in Somerset, but she doesn't speak to him for reasons I'm not old enough to know yet, so he doesn't really count. My mother had three younger brothers in all: Jack-Rogers, Eugene, and Joseph. Like most people in southwestern Pennsylvania, they had nicknames. Jack-Rogers, the oldest of the three, goes by "Roger." Eugene, the middle brother, was known as "Boots," and Joseph, the youngest, was called "Little Joe." Boots and Little Joe both died in sad ways before I was born—one beaten to death during a drunken fight on a naval ship,

4

one liver-poisoned from too much nerve medicine. I picture my uncle Boots drinking it straight from a brown glass bottle with no label, then counting the money in his sock drawer. My mother says when Boots died, she found two thousand dollars in that drawer, all in nickels and dimes. She talks about Boots and Little Joe like they're still alive, her eyes moist and shiny, her cheeks suddenly a brighter pink as if blood is trying to pump itself out of her through invisible holes in her skin.

I peel myself from the wet summer grass of our backyard and wander inside the house through the large sliding-glass door. Every night before we go to bed, my mother closes the slider, then puts a stick in the door. It's a piece of broom handle my father cut and shaped to fit in the grooves of the door's sliding track, so no one can break in while we sleep. We call that piece of wood the-stick-in-the-door. We like to name things based on where they belong, like the-pen-by-the-phone, my mother's black Bic ballpoint that lives in a small orange box of scrap paper next to the kitchen telephone. You better not move the-pen-by-the-phone, not even an inch, or there will be hell to pay, even though I've discovered my mother has entire packages of those pens stashed in the attic.

My father is in the kitchen—dark blue work jacket, collar up to his ears, his black lunch box symbolizing departure. Hungry cats circle the yellow rug as he makes wax paper–wrapped sandwiches, loads small cakes wrapped in cellophane, and stores the Coca-Cola he drinks, a bottle an hour, to stay awake. He is working the night shift tonight at Anchor Glass, the glass factory in the south end of town. I don't say *goodbye* to him, convinced that if I do he will somehow die before 7:00 a.m., will not return to this brick home on this slanted street, these windows secured with shiny brass locks. I say *good night* instead, running through my catalog of different ways it can happen: heart attack, explosion, a fall into the furnace. I sleep in bed with my mother when he's gone, check the-stick-in-the-door eight times before I try to fall asleep, listen to our house settle in the night.

"But our house isn't very old. Why does it settle?" I ask my mother.

"It's stretching itself out. You know, getting used to the land," she says, half asleep already. At 7:00 a.m., she will begin her shift at Anchor Glass just as my father punches a stiff time card into a clock and walks up the long metal staircase that leads out of the underground furnace. My older sister Linda and I are big enough to sleep alone in the house for the fifteen minutes that pass between my mother's departure and my father's arrival.

I wake to the sound of my mother closing the front door—the soft thud the swollen wood releases, the *ka-ching* of the screen door. I run down the hallway but only manage to catch the back of her platinum-blond head as she walks briskly to her car, the used maroon Lincoln with vinyl seats that stick to our bare legs in summer.

Linda sleeps in her own bedroom, shaded by stiff burgundy drapes. She breathes in and out with a whistle, clutches her stuffed Pink Panther. She's sewn a line of odd buttons down his tail. Linda's bedroom furniture is ivory with antique-looking handles. She has a skinny chest of drawers taller than me, in which she keeps socks of every color imaginable. My mother arranges them in hues: reds, oranges, and yellows in the bottom drawers; blues and greens in the top drawers; neutrals in the middle. I open the drawers slowly, let the rows of color dizzy me, then close each one quietly.

I go back to my own room with the pink ballerina bed skirt with walls painted to match. I put one eye up to the slit between the window curtain panels, holding the other eye shut with a finger. I watch for a brown and white Chevy Blazer, and when it pulls up to the curb, I make sure it's my father who gets out. He always comes home in one piece; mesh cap perched on his shiny black hair. I knock three times on the wooden window frame, slide down under my covers, and pretend to sleep.

★ ★ ★

According to the FBI, mass murder is defined as four or more murders occurring during a particular event with no cooling-off period between them. A mass murder typically occurs in a single location, three or more victims killed by one individual. When you're eight years old, definitions make sense. You know how to look things up in your family's fancy set of Britannica Encyclopedias, the rows of books that sleep in a wooden shelf next to the piano your sister plays. The pages are bible-thin and edged with gold, an effect that is only visible when the book is closed.

I'm in second grade. My teacher, Mrs. Swan, sends weekly newsletters home from school. When she signs her name, she draws a small beak on the capital *S* in her name, draws a row of ocean waves underneath, stiff peaks and low rockers. Ever since we learned how to write in cursive, I see serifs everywhere. I'm left-handed, so I'm taught to slant my paper and hold my pencil in a certain way. Left-handers are notorious for sloppy penmanship, but not me. Mrs. Swan praises my daily writing exercises. My hooks and stems are perfect. One day she invites Mrs. Lambert, the other second-grade teacher, to come watch me write that day's message on a yellow sheet of paper. *Today is Tuesday, March 5, 1985. McDonald's is opening in Connellsville today. We have our own golden arches now!*

Last summer, in California, a man named James O. Huberty walked into a McDonald's near San Diego and started shooting. He killed twenty-one people and himself. On *20/20*, Hugh Downs and Barbara Walters described the event, but they didn't include the perpetrator in death counts. The killer is always separate. He (it's usually he, but I know women kill people, too) doesn't deserve to be in the same group as the victims, even though they're all dead now and how could it possibly matter whether or not you place their names together in print, whether you speak their names in the same sentence? I understand the emotion of it, how the victims' families need that separation between the murderer and the murdered, but I sometimes feel sorry for the killers, and that makes me wonder if there's something wrong with me.

Every day, Mrs. Swan draws lines on the chalkboard with a five-prong wooden chalk holder. She starts on the left side and walks across to the right, her shoes making hard sounds on the terrazzo floor. The lines turn the chalkboard into a sheet of notebook paper, and she writes our daily writing on it. We copy her sentences, then she collects our papers, returns them to us the following day, with notes of encouragement or rubber stamps of red ink smiley faces. After daily writing, we stand for the pledge of allegiance, then bow our heads for a moment of silence. We recite the seven continents as Mrs. Swan points to each on a world map she pulls from a blue metal canister above the chalkboard. We practice our directions—north, south, east, and west. Even in second grade, it's important to know how to read a map, to know where you're going. James O. Huberty's apartment was only three blocks from the McDonald's in San Diego. He didn't need a map.

Connellsville, Pennsylvania, where I've lived all of my eight years, is a small city on the Youghiogheny River. We call it the Yough for short. It's pronounced with a hard *k* sound *(Yock),* and it's usually high and muddy. There's an arched bridge that crosses the Yough and when we drive over it, I watch for fishermen, men in rubber waders like my father, who stand at the edge of the bank and cast invisible lines for fish. The men don't move much—they are still as statues. My mother can't understand why my father enjoys spending hours in muddy water up to his waist. He sews carpet on the soles of his waders, his special technique to avoid slipping on the rocks.

Trout season starts in April each year. My father will fish the Yough a few times, but he prefers Dunbar Creek (which we pronounce *crick*). On days off from the factory, he wakes before dawn and sets out with his old yellow cooler, his salvaged plastic bread bags (for holding cleaned fish), his milk jugs of frozen water (make-shift ice packs), his fly rod and reel. Baby food jars hold salmon eggs; old Cool Whip and butter containers house live meal worms, holes poked in the lids so you can smell them, the sawdust they burrow into, their bodies curled tightly inside. Do they know their place in the food chain? I hope they don't feel a thing when my father slides one onto a hook, that little bubble of pus oozing out.

My father tells made-up stories to Linda and me at bedtime, when our mother works the night shift. We beg him to tell us these stories over and over again, so much so that we finally convince him to record them on our Sears tape recorder, so we can hear his stories any time we want, calling his voice into the air from a thin spool of tape that winds around our plastic Memorex cassette. He tells his own version of *The Three Little Pigs*. In his version there's a cool pig, a serious pig, and a stuttering pig. He also tells us tales of a young boy named Egglebert Humperdinky, whose life, I begin to notice, resembles my father's. Egglebert has three older sisters—Betty, Barbara, and Becky. He lives in a small village in the woods where he and his brother get into trouble.

In my favorite story, Egglebert visits an old village man named Mr. Kovach. Mr. Kovach tells of a spirit called The Shadow that appears in the woods on certain nights around midnight. The Shadow makes a clicking sound, that's how you know it's there. Mr. Kovach says that when he was a boy, he heard that sound one night, as he lay in his bed half asleep. He ran outside to see what it was and in the woods behind his house he saw a light, like a dim lantern, moving along a path. He followed and followed the light for nearly a mile, when suddenly it disappeared. *Poof.* The light just went out. This happened several nights in a row, until finally Mr. Kovach decided to begin marking the spot where the light disappeared. It turned out that the light went out at the exact same spot in the woods each and every night.

Mr. Kovach decided to dig in that spot and sure enough, he found a real honest to goodness ruby in the ground—The Shadow's treasure. Egglebert Humperdinky becomes obsessed with the legend of The Shadow. He lies awake night after night listening for the clicking sound, until finally he hears it. Each time my father tells the story, Egglebert finds a different treasure when he digs in that spot in the dark woods—a velvet bag full of pearls, a stack of gold coins, a raw diamond.

After the stories are over, my father goes down to the basement to watch the local news and Johnny Carson. I sit at the top of the stairs and listen to Johnny's theme song play as he appears from the rainbow-colored curtain that I'm sure would feel like real silk if only I could touch it. Later, I lie in my bed perfectly still, so the ruffles on my bedspread don't make a sound. I want to be silent, so I hold my breath in as long as I can and listen for The Shadow, the steady clicking sound that must resemble a beating heart. I never hear it, just my own breath when I finally exhale.

★ ★ ★

My sister Linda, her friend Rochelle, and I are in Linda's bedroom—red shag carpet, cream furniture with fake antique handles, the walls textured, thick with layers of white paint. The windows hide behind heavy red curtains, the kind of drapes you open with a rope and pulley system, a dozen sharp metal hooks we're forbidden to touch.

We're huddled around a French telephone, its elegant mouthpiece curved like an ivory horn.

"Just do it, already," Linda commands.

"You do it. It's your idea," I say.

Rochelle laughs through her nose. She's lying on her side, propped up on one arm, fingering the three-inch mass of neon jelly bracelets on her wrist. "You're scared," she says.

"I am not!" I insist. I'm sitting cross-legged on the floor, inspecting the shiny pennies in my cordovan loafers. My mother taught me that color—cordovan. It just looks like burgundy to me.

We're trying to prove a rumor going around our elementary school: If you dial 666 on your telephone, the devil will answer.

"Not necessarily the devil himself," Rochelle explains. "You could get one of his helpers." She tugs on her chewing gum until it breaks, snapping her chin, a sticky string of pale pink dangling.

"The devil has helpers?" I ask. "Like Santa's elves?"

"Sure, something like that," Linda says, giving Rochelle a look, as if to say *she's impossible,* mimicking my mother's expression when I ask too many questions.

"Okay, but what do I say when he picks up?" I need to know.

"Just say, *sorry, wrong number,*" Rochelle says.

I imagine telephone lines sleeping in the ground, red and yellow and black, spiderlike fingers stretched beneath earth. The devil sits in a leather chair, somewhere in hell. I grab the receiver from its pearly cradle, and dial.

★ ★ ★

My mother is a storyteller, too, but she tells true stories. Some stories belong to others, and she tells them, over and over again, because my mother knows the shape of suffering. She tells me about a young man who is about to propose to his high school sweetheart. He's driven to her house hundreds of times over the years, but on this particular night, he drives with a diamond ring in his pocket, a crushed velvet box that will surely open with a creak as he kneels in front of her in her parents' living room, in her childhood home on Christmas Eve, turkey or ham in the oven, glazed with butter or honey or brown sugar. On this night, the most important night of this young life, the man loses control of his car on the icy street, the one he's driven too many times to count, really, and he is thrown from the vehicle, splashing through the windshield and onto the inky pavement on a night without a moon, for it is certain that most bad things happen during a new moon. When the police arrive, they find him face-down, the diamond ring, somehow freed from its box, glittering on the frozen pavement beside him.

In another story, a teenage girl wakes up on the morning of her birthday. She is a spoiled girl, and she's asked for a pair of brown suede boots for her birthday, expects them gift-wrapped and waiting for her at the breakfast table. Instead, her father presents her with a card. There is no money inside, no sign of the suede boots. The girl screams at her father, storms out the kitchen door and off to school, *drop dead,* her words to her father, echoing over her shoulder. A few hours later, the girl's father has a massive heart attack and dies. When the girl returns home later that evening, after spending the day at the hospital with her mother and dead father, she finds a pink box on her bed, tied in red ribbon. Inside, under tissue paper that crinkles, she finds the brown suede boots. Her father had them all along.

Some stories belong to my mother, if it's possible to own a story, to carry it inside a small case you wear, perhaps one that fits neatly inside your shoe, invisible to most people. She only takes the stories out of the case for me, not Linda, not my father, not the women she talks to on the phone. Just me. Sometimes, I feel like the stories were written just for me, so that maybe I can carry a small case of my own stories some day, so I will remember the shape of suffering.

When my mother was born, she came out wrong. No, she didn't slide out feet first—she was a girl. According to her father, she was supposed to be a boy. It was 1941 and my mother was the first child of JR and Pearl Richter. My grandfather, whose full name was Jack-Rogers Richter, wanted nothing to do with a daughter. In fact, he didn't even lay eyes on my mother until she was seven years old.

My mother, little Gloria (who would later be nicknamed Ginny by her high school classmates who decided her name was ugly, making people eternally assume in error that her given name is Virginia) was whisked away to her grandmother Lindermann's house. Granny Lindermann was Pearl's mother. She lived alone just a few blocks from JR and Pearl.

Everyone in Connellsville remembers my grandfather. When he was out and about, he was the big talker, the big spender, the big joker. At home, he was the big drinker, the big fighter. Pearl wore long sleeves even on the hottest summer days, and everyone in the house came to dread Sunday nights, when he would be the most drunk, the most wild, the most dangerous. My mother remembers hiding under overturned mattresses, covering Pearl's bruises with heavy pancake makeup. She remembers Pearl hanging wet wash on the clothesline in freezing weather because the electricity had been shut off for nonpayment and JR had been missing for two weeks, leaving no money in the house for them to live on.

When my mother was born, JR exiled her to Granny Lindermann's and didn't bat an eye. He and Pearl went on to have three more children—all sons—and seemed to be just fine without little Gloria until Granny Lindermann died when my mom was seven years old. Of course, she was sent back to live with her parents, to meet her little brothers for the first time, and to finally meet her father. Pearl had visited my mother secretly a few times.

My mother remembers sitting on the porch on Atlas Avenue crying and crying into a handkerchief. She was so scared to go home. I think of this scene now and I want to reach down into the well of time and somehow hold my mother close, closer than she'd ever let me be in real life—to smell her hair, to let her bury her head on my shoulder, while I whisper in her ear. *Mommy, I wish you didn't have to go.*

My father is from Lemont Furnace, a village in the foothills of the Laurel Mountains. My father's family lived in a valley known unofficially as Yauger Hollow. Residents pronounce it *Yaga Halla.* This kind of thing makes my mother cringe, her eyebrows wrinkling like angry caterpillars, her mouth pursing into a painful-looking sneer. "They might as well call it Dog Patch," she says. My mother doesn't exactly come from high class herself, but her father did go to college, and he worked as an engineer on the CSX Railroad. My parents occasionally engage in a friendly game of Who Was Poorest Growing Up, but my father always wins quickly and easily as soon as the subject of indoor plumbing comes up or something like churning one's own butter or cleaning your clothes by hitting rocks against them in a stream.

My father grew up in a house that his father built with his own hands. The rooms didn't have regular doors that closed. Instead, they had curtains that were hung from thin rods or, in some cases, just pinned over the doorway with straight pins. My mother grew up in a house the size of a funeral home—rooms and rooms with hardwood floors and beveled windows and a wraparound porch. The house is so big, it is now being converted into four apartments, and although the paint is peeling and the wooden pillars in front have been whittled down by the rain and the wind, it is still a grand house. The old place is in South Connellsville, not far from Anchor, so we must pass it as we drive along Pittsburgh Street on our way to drop someone off or pick someone up from work.

Weekends were horrible times for my mother as a child. Her father drank from sundown Friday to sundown Sunday, dragging himself to his railroad job on Monday mornings. My mother learned to hate Sundays most of all, for this was when her father was the most drunk, when objects sailed around the room, when the children tried to stand in front of their mother, a movable living shield. To this day my mother hates Sundays and feels a quiet release of joy when she wakes up and it's finally Monday morning. She remembers this feeling in her bones, has carried it all this way, all these years, to me.

My mother wears these stories, and others. They live somewhere inside her. My mother is a well and these stories spring from her. She can control when they come out. She gives me a sprinkle here and there, a small dollop of sadness when I need it, when I forget about suffering, about our history. *Don't let yourself be happy, because that's when it will find you.* The stories will always find me, just as they have always found my mother.

Some stories end. They end and exist in a space where things are final. They won't be told again because you've already learned from that story. You know what the story knows. But other stories, they never end. Instead, they continue to grow, continue to be told, the feelings in them felt over and over, a living, breathing part of you, an organ, like skin or a lung. Sometimes, you can stand there and watch your own history inflate like a balloon. If you let it go, it will fly into the air, and you can watch it get smaller and smaller, watch its slanted path, its white ribbon tail waving surrender as the balloon becomes a quarter, a nickel, a penny, a dime, then nothing at all.

# CHAPTER 2

# Throw Salt over Your Shoulder

Bad things are happening everywhere in 1985, but never here, never in Connellsville. We can look out and see the bad things happening. We can read newspaper articles and watch news reports. Sometimes we can even feel the bad things, just sense them—a general idea of doom. Sometimes I feel like I'm a tiny pebble in a river, and bad things wash over my body and I can only lie there and watch, the bad things rubbing against me, taking bits of me with them, like the process of erosion we learn about in Earth Science class. We are surrounded by river here, by streams and creeks. Water is trickling somewhere right now, even if you can't hear it, can't make out the slight ticking of it all. Water is alive; my father knows this. He studies water temperature, currents, high-water marks around bridges. He studies the fish under the water, too, knows when they're spawning, when they're more likely to eat from a hook.

I am scared for my father when he's out fishing. He doesn't even know how to swim, yet there he'll be, chest-high in a dark river, wearing rubber overalls, his fishing license tacked to the back of his cap with a large safety pin. I worry about a lot of things for him, not just drowning, which is a recurring nightmare. I've seen my father's bloated body pulled from the river in my dreams. I've seen him laid out on a metal drawer in a morgue; I've seen a tag tied to his big toe. I worry about someone robbing him, about poisonous snakes attacking him, his heart giving out suddenly. I've seen him clutching his chest and collapsing into a pile of wet leaves on a riverbank. I worry about a crazed murderer jumping off the train at the station in Connellsville, right next to the river bank, right there on River Street, which flooded once, and became its name.

Ted Bundy did something like that. He took a bus as far as he could, which turned out to be Gainesville, Florida, and that's where he bludgeoned two college girls to death in their bedrooms that must have been decorated the way girls' rooms tend to be decorated. Posters taped to the walls and bundles of dried flowers hanging upside down. What's stopping someone like that from coming here? What makes this the place where nothing bad ever happens? People always think bad things won't happen to them. What makes us *them?*

My visions are deep and colorful, full of senses. I can smell my dreams, taste them sometimes, wake with my mouth still full of dreams. I don't tell anyone, though, just keep it to myself. My mother says you should never talk about a dream before you've eaten breakfast, unless you want it to come true. I'm not sure why yet, but our town feels guilty. It feels like there's something we've done, and even we don't know what it is.

I look up the word bludgeon in the dictionary, wonder why it only seems to be used for a certain kind of beating. The entry says *bludgeon: verb [trans.] beat (someone) repeatedly with a bludgeon or other heavy object.* The person is placed in parentheses, to separate the victim from the one who beats, the one who kills. Our parents don't hit us the way their own parents hit them. My father was whipped with switches from trees, my mother with belts and I'm not sure what else. They say they would never want to hurt us that way. I know kids who get spanked at home, get paddled at school by the principal, Mr. Hamacher.

We call it getting "cracks," and Jimmy Carter holds the record for the most cracks in one sitting. He's a chatty boy, unrelated to the ex-president, with red hair and freckles who looks like Howdy Doody, buckteeth and all. Jimmy and I are related by marriage on my father's side. Something about my father's second cousin marrying his father's third cousin. It's very remote, but Jimmy talks about it all the time to embarrass me. Me being the good little girl and him being the one who holds the record for cracks.

★ ★ ★

In our family, when we play Monopoly, we each have a favorite game piece. My father is the horse, reared back as if ready to gallop, front legs bent in midair. My mother is the iron. She likes to press anything she can get her hands on—jeans, T-shirts, even the red and blue paisley handkerchiefs my father blows his nose into. Linda is the car, an old-fashioned racer that reminds me of the turnpike ride at Kennywood Park in Pittsburgh. The cars let you believe you're steering, when really they run along a thin metal rail so you can never crash. I am the little Scotty dog, ears and tail pointing up, ready to follow you at a moment's notice.

Like most families, we covet Boardwalk and Park Place. If my mother buys them, she'll build giant towers on them like Donald Trump, the real estate tycoon who is one of her idols. When she finds out Donald has a little boy around my age, Donald Jr., she concocts a plan for he and I to marry someday. Then I can whisk her away from factory life, and she can get a job at the Estée Lauder counter, selling creamy blush and tubes of jet-black mascara, wands that look like small caterpillars and make a soft sound when you slide them out of their shiny cases.

I like to look at the "luxury tax" square, that shiny diamond ring glistening from the game board. My mother has a small diamond ring, but she never wears it. You can't wear rings at the factory because jewelry can get caught in the machinery, make you lose a finger, or even a chunk of your hand. Penny Horvac, my mother's friend from C crew, comes over sometimes, and I try not to stare at the nubs of what used to be her middle and pinky fingers, resting on the orange vinyl tablecloth as she smokes with her good hand.

Linda collects green houses whenever possible, builds red hotels that look like fire erupting across her corner of the game board. My father always says something when he rolls the dice. *Daddy needs a new pair of shoes* or *Come on seven.* His chants usually seem to work, so I try it, too. When it's not her turn, my mother looks off into the distance through the sliding-glass door, tilts her head toward the kitchen to check the time on the clock above the harvest-gold stove. It's her turn to work the night shift tonight, so she's counting down the minutes until seven o'clock, when she'll disappear into her bedroom and rest in darkness for three hours. The rest of us must go down to the basement during that time, and we mustn't breathe too loudly or jump around, until ten o'clock. At that time, my mother emerges to prepare herself for work, a sliver of light under the bathroom door to indicate she is awake.

I sit on the fuzzy blue toilet seat cover and watch her get ready. She coats her face and neck with a cotton ball soaked in beige liquid makeup, rubs her cheeks with a dab of lipstick instead of blush, sets her hair in hot rollers, and finishes the look with a heavy mist of both Adorn aerosol hairspray and Youth Dew perfume. I like the dizzy feeling I get from the fumes, thinking this is what it must feel like to be drunk.

The factory is called Anchor Glass, and it's mostly underground, at the south end of town. The only building you can see from the street is the office. It is made of tan brick with pale stone columns, like it belongs in *Clash of the Titans.* Inside the factory, beneath the earth, people make glass containers—bottles, jars, jugs—vessels that will eventually hold vinegar, beer, baby food, mustard, all the staples of life. My father works in an area called The Hot End. This is where they keep the furnaces, where my father sweats in dark blue coveralls, his name sewn on a patch over his heart. He shovels a black sand mixture called batch into the ovens, where it melts into molds stamped with numbers that come out raised like Braille. I'm sure everything glows orange and red in the dark of The Hot End. I imagine my father holding a hot branding rod as if he's about to mark a steer. I see horns, the animal struggling, hear a low moan, exhale.

My mother works in The Cold End. Despite its name, the temperature in this area of the factory hovers somewhere in the neighborhood of eighty degrees, but that's nothing compared to The Hot End, where my father works in triple-digit heat. In The Cold End, my mother works as a selector. She works with longneck green bottles that will eventually become Rolling Rock beer bottles once they leave Anchor Glass and are shipped to the brewing company in nearby Latrobe, Pennsylvania. The bottles run on conveyor belt lines, and they are automatically tested during their journey with various pieces of machinery. One of the tests is a plunger test, which simulates the bottle being filled with liquid. It's designed to determine whether or not the bottle is strong enough to withstand the pressure of filling. My mother supervises the machinery, like a glass babysitter of sorts. She pulls samples off the line for quality assurance, tests them for consistency, so they are uniform. No bottle should be unique.

Years ago, the factory made a now-discontinued line of tableware—rose-colored plates and cups and saucers. They called it Roseware, and you could see through it, almost like looking through a pair of glasses, to see a happier world on the other side.

There are things we can't talk about in this house, not because someone has told us we can't, but because no one has told us we can. In our world, in the child world, most everything is black or white, love or hate, rest or play. There is seldom a middle place. You are either in Mother's way or she doesn't see you at all. Her line of sight runs straight through people's hearts. Bodies become invisible, and the most important ones are dead in the ground or rotting in a mausoleum off Route 119. My grandparents are buried there, not in dirt, but in stone drawers. I read in a magazine once that hair and fingernails continue to grow after death, picture my grandmother with wild gray strands thin as wire, my grandfather's toenails yellow and curled. I swear to Linda that I would open one of those drawers if I could. She dares me, double dares, double dog dares.

At the change of each season, we put the little black stool in the trunk of the Lincoln and drive to the cemetery, where my mother climbs out and uses the stool to retrieve memorial vases full of silk flowers from the burial chambers. She takes them to DeMath's Florist in town, has a woman named Tibby create a new arrangement to fit the new season. Sunflowers for summer, mums for fall, poinsettias for winter, lilies for spring. I like to pull the old flowers out of the vases, to release the plastic stems from green foam that used to be spongy but now crumbles, dried out from the winds on top of that hill where the mausoleum looks down on the highway, no lights to guide you there at night. You just have to know where it is. You just have to know that your family is sleeping there, behind golden nameplates wearing tiny days, months, and years.

★ ★ ★

I throw salt over my shoulder when I spill some. I stay up on New Year's Eve to eat grapes at midnight.

The idea is that if you eat twelve grapes at midnight on New Year's Eve, you will have good luck for the year. You have to eat the grapes during the twelve strokes of midnight, one grape for each month of the upcoming year. Any less and you'll risk an incomplete cycle of luck. If you only eat eleven, you'll have one month of disaster. And if that isn't bad enough, you won't know which month it will be.

To my mother, good luck equals money. She has many strategies for me to become rich. She instructs me to drink as many milk bubbles as I can because each bubble represents one hundred dollars I'll have as an adult. I can't wait for the milk jug to be nearly empty, because I know most bubbles live at the bottom. When my mother pours the last bit into my cup, I chug greedily, and she smiles.

There are lots of superstitions about good luck and prosperity. Shaking an empty purse at the full moon is thought to bring riches. The first time I do it, I'm disappointed because I think actual money will appear in the purse the next morning. I wake up and race to the small leather purse, a gift my father had brought back from a hunting trip in New Mexico, dissolving into tears when faced with its emptiness.

But my mother assures me that superstitions aren't magic. They can't make things happen *immediately*. "They're like insurance," she explains. "Sometimes you need to do certain things to make sure bad things won't happen. And other times you need to do certain things to give good things a helping hand."

I can control the world by following these superstitions and by counting things. I count the sips of water I drink at the school water fountain, the number of jelly beans I eat (it's unlucky to eat an odd number), the seconds I spend washing my hands. I knock on wood after most thoughts. Throughout the day, I keep track of all the knocks I owe the universe, then run to the bathroom and knock over and over again on the wooden door of the linen closet that holds neatly folded bath towels, families of shampoo bottles, and bars of soap in beautiful rows.

If our house is a body, the kitchen is the heart, full of dark flesh, full of blood. It's where my father prepares gutted fish for dinner, where he grinds raw deer meat into burger, cuts liver into thin slices.

He wraps it all in foil, labels the packages with a fat black permanent marker, the kind kids at school say you can sniff and get high from the fumes. Every year in November, our kitchen becomes a butcher shop, the metallic smell of animal blood thick in the air. The grinder is loud as it tears apart deer muscle, my father tamping slabs of red meat from the feed pan into the tube with his bare hands. The ground meat oozes from the holes through various dies, like our Play-Doh Fun Factory. You can make your own shapes, mold it into anything your want.

My father grinds the meat into a giant glass bowl and then breaks it into one-pound servings for future spaghetti sauce, chili, meatloaf. We don't eat beef in this house. Everything you would make with beef, we make with deer meat. Linda and I like to fool our visiting friends into eating it, assuring them they're eating pieces of cow in their chili. Only after they've cleaned their bowl, sopped up every delicious bit with their buttered English muffin, do we reveal the truth. "*You just ate Bambi!*" we like to tease.

Our kitchen is also the place where the sweets are stored—packaged cookies and snack cakes that my sister and I eat in large quantities. We'll split an entire box of Twinkies, unwrapping new ones while the last ones are still in our mouths, the way chain-smokers light a new cigarette with the end of an old one. We'll eat a whole package of Oreos, dunking them in a Tupperware bowl of milk. We'll eat store-bought frosting from the can, brown sugar by the spoonful. Anything sweet goes directly into our waiting mouths. Afterward, we'll lie on the couch in the basement holding our sides, half asleep on sugar, but feeling half loved, too.

When my mother works the afternoon shift, she has to leave for the factory right before we come home from school. I'll enter the house, throw my book bag on the floor, and run to the kitchen to find meatloaf and potatoes baking in the oven, a pot of candied carrots on a back burner, bubbling in a glaze of brown sugar sauce.

There are wire racks of oatmeal raisin cookies on the counter, still warm to the touch. In the bathroom, her perfume and hairspray are still in the air, a fine mist that coats the blue edges of the sink, leaves spots of residue on the mirror. I see myself in the mirror, but also see her. We have the same prominent nose, the same heart-shaped face. Her hair is blond now, but it used to be dark brown like mine. In the girl factory, something must have gone wrong. I look like my mother on the outside, but not the inside.

★ ★ ★

I know things. I don't know how I know them, but I do. I know that if I rub my finger against my underwear, right there in the middle of me, something happens. Sometimes I can't stand doing it because it scares me and sometimes I think I might break myself, but I can't stand not doing it, either. The idea of it teases me as I lay in my bed at night. The house is dark and quiet, not even my parents whispering from their room or sounds of the television from Linda's little white thirteen-inch set. The moment feels like it will last forever, yet when it's over it feels unreal, dreamlike. Did it really happen at all? How can something that feels so big last for only an instant? I don't know what it's really called, but in my mind I call it reaching the dew point.

We've been learning about weather in school, about the water cycle, how rain evaporates, becomes the soft white bodies of clouds, how steam condenses into water, how the process never ends. The dew point is the temperature to which air must be cooled for water vapor to condense into water and make dew. It's almost springtime, and when I walk to school in the morning, there are globes of dew on the stiff grass, the bright green sod my mother had the landscaping men put down so that we would always have a beautiful lawn.

My father wanted to start a vegetable garden out back, like the kind he and his siblings tended to as a child in Yaga Halla. "In the summertime, between the garden and my fishing, I can catch and grow most of our food," he said. "Your mom will barely have to go to the grocery store." My mother vetoed the idea, mouthed the words "Dog Patch" to me behind his back, rolled her eyes beneath lashes clumped with too much black mascara. I remember watching the landscaping company dig up the yard and then roll out the sod like carpet, long strands they cut to size so my mother wouldn't have to look at brown grass because she doesn't like dead things, only dead people.

Surely, I must have my own temperature, surely part of me can evaporate, can rise up into the sky and become a cloud. This is what I think about when I rub the washed cotton of my underwear against that spot, the center of me. The water, the vapor, the clouds. The water, the vapor, the clouds.

There are three basic types of clouds—cumulus, stratus, cirrus— and I write a report about them for school, make a small book cover for it out of blue construction paper, cotton glued to the front in the shape of my favorite clouds, cumulus. They are fair-weather clouds, mid to low level, and if you see them, you know it will be a beautiful day. Some days in Connellsville, there are no clouds at all. Those days make me nervous, the way my mother gets nervous when I hover around her. She wants the air near her clean, free of little girls and our milky breath, our braids slapping against our backs when we walk.

Mother insists on doing my hair every day. Barrettes, headbands, side ponytails, or a straight part down the middle and two braids so tight you can see my clean pink scalp, a perfect line dissecting my dark head. My head feels sore at night, when my hair is finally freed, hanging in crimped waves down to my waist. When I attempt to part my hair myself, my mother says it's as crooked as a dog's hind leg. I spend a long time looking in the mirror that hangs above my pressboard dresser, trying to tame my hair into that perfect part, licking the comb to taste the oil, that faint animal smell, the only way I recognize myself.

# CHAPTER 3

# Into the Eyes of the Devil Standing There

Trees around the blue factory fence pull moisture from the ground. Their roots are thin reeds sucking water, desperate to bloom. A sparrow in love perches on my low windowsill, listening to rain in his sleep. It's a Friday in 1985, two days before St. Patrick's Day, and everywhere, the muddy signs of spring present themselves. I am still eight years old and the world is perfect, for now.

In Mrs. Swan's second-grade class we're cutting out shamrocks—green construction paper so coarse you can see the grain. Mrs. Swan is tall and thin. She speaks in that voice only elementary school teachers have. The school scissors are dull metal with red rubber covering the circles where your fingers belong. Our classroom is decorated with paper lions and lambs because March comes in like a lion, and out like a lamb. At the beginning of the month, we were able to choose which one we wanted to make. I chose a lamb and got to use cotton balls for her wool, pink crayons for the soft insides of her ears.

I want to be a meteorologist when I grow up, so I like sayings that deal with the weather. When my father was my age, they didn't have weathermen on TV. They didn't even have TV. They had to look at the sky to see if rain was coming, had to lick a finger and raise it in the air to find the direction of the wind. Now my father loves weather reports. He loves barometers and thermometers, low-pressure systems and cold fronts, nimbus clouds and hail and blizzards. He loves watching the radar picture on the evening news. I stare at the animated green and white mass as it moves over the tristate area, the outline of West Virginia's panhandle a little chimney, dividing us from Ohio.

That night, I watch the eleven o'clock news with my father. His favorite station is KDKA, the oldest news station in the country, broadcast from Pittsburgh, fifty-seven miles away. In Pittsburgh, people break into houses that look a lot like ours—brick ranches with porches and wooden fences, front yards with bare trees, branches like bony fingers reaching into the sky. But our city is smaller, a small doll nesting inside larger cities, protected. Nothing bad ever happens here.

"This town is dying," my mother announces. "But you're smart, Karen. And you'll get out of here when you're older. An Ivy League graduate won't want to live around a bunch of goddamned has-beens."

My mother has already decided that I'll attend Harvard, Yale, or Princeton. She pictures me becoming a female version of Lee Iacocca, the CEO of Chrysler. Lee Iacocca is from Allentown, proof that you can rise above the mines and mills of Pennsylvania and make something of yourself. Another acceptable alternative would be to marry the son of Andrew Mellon, from the rich Pittsburgh family that owns Mellon Bank.

"After you two get married, they'll have to change the jingle to *Karen Bank, a neighbor you can count on*," she sings as she twirls around in our orange and gold kitchen, the mushroom curtains dancing with her in the damp breeze.

The factory work schedule is taped to the wall next to the harvest-gold telephone that matches the harvest-gold refrigerator and stove, and the mushroom canisters that were in style in the 1970s, when I was born. When something important comes up, either Linda or I have to check the schedule—a long skinny paper creased a million times, encoded in cryptic letters and numbers, a mysterious eye chart. I run my finger down, tracing the days of my dance recital, my chorus concert, my birthday. First I have to determine if one of my parents is off that day. If not, the second step is to decide who will call off work, and that's usually my mother. I'm told that since my father makes more money, it makes sense for him to work as much as possible. But even if that's true, we all know the real reason and that is simple—Mother is in charge. She controls every aspect of our home life—from which brand of paper towels to buy, to which trees to pay the landscaper to plant in the yard, to whether or not we answer the door when the doorbell rings unexpectedly on a Saturday afternoon.

I don't need to consult the work schedule much lately, because my father isn't working right now. He's on sick leave from the factory because he's having *bowel trouble* as my mother puts it. He's going to doctor's appointments at a big hospital in Pittsburgh, where they put scopes and tubes and needles in him, run test after test. So far, they think he might be lactose intolerant, so my mother buys lactose-free milk for him. My father is a big milk drinker, at least three glasses with every meal, and he hates the taste of the lactose-free version, refusing to drink it after a few sips. "I only like the real thing," he says. "That's why I won't drink that new Coke, either."

So far, even after giving up milk, he's still got *the trouble,* the family nickname for his sickness right now. It keeps him in the bathroom most of the day, a stack of fishing magazines on the floor next to the toilet. Even though my mother thinks it's tacky to have reading materials in the bathroom, she's letting it slide this time.

My mother tells me family secrets, and one of them is that dad's sickness is just nerves. One of the foremen at the factory gave him a hard time recently, scolded him, saying something vague like "I don't like the way you move." While my father doesn't like to speak up for himself, my mother is the opposite. She is loud and opinionated and doesn't let people "shit all over her." She thinks my oldest sister, Pam, is a pushover, a doormat.

"She takes so much shit, she should just change her name to Pam Brown," my mother says. Pam is mom's daughter from her first marriage, and she's fifteen years older than me. Pam got married one week after her high school graduation and moved out of the house. I was only three years old then, so I grew up seeing Pam as a second mother instead of a sister. I took to calling her "Mama Pam Pam." Pam and her husband, Luke, were high school sweethearts. They only stayed married for three years, long enough to have a little girl named Samantha, who is my niece, even though she's only four years younger than me.

My father adopted Pam when he and my mother got married. Pam's real father is a man named Leroy who lives in Indiana. My mother doesn't talk about him much, but when she does, she says Leroy cheated on her with other women and has probably fathered close to a dozen children himself, although he's never remarried. My father likes to tell the story about how he rescued my mom and Pam. When my dad came over to their apartment for the first time, they had only ketchup in their refrigerator. He showed up the next day with two sacks full of groceries.

My father is shy; so shy that he didn't even have the nerve to ask my mother out on a date thirteen years ago. According to the story, my mother approached one of my dad's friends at the end of her shift and said, "Tell Charles I want a date with him!" And that was that. My father was thirty-five at the time and still living at home in the hollow with my grandmother Zelda and his sister, my aunt Babe.

Nicknames are mandatory in my father's family. He is "Manny" to anyone who knew him before he married my mother. He was given that nickname as a child, because everyone thought he acted just like a little man. My father has three older sisters and one younger brother whose nickname is Honeyboy. Honeyboy is a big man with a long reddish brown beard like the guys from the band ZZ Top. He looks gruff and mean but inside he's a softie. He has a dog named Booey (who also has a nickname, Hutch). He teaches Hutch tricks. When my dad takes Linda and me to visit Honeyboy, he shows us how Hutch can identify the various stuffed wildlife on the wood-paneled walls of his small den.

Honeyboy says, "*Where's* the turkey?" taking care to hold out the word *where's* like an auctioneer, and Hutch's golden-haired head snaps, turns abruptly to look at the wild turkey feathers spread out and nailed to the wall like a giant fan. "*Where's* the deer?" Honeyboy asks, and Hutch looks at the sad mounted dear head, its neck disappearing as if the rest of its body could be found inside the wall, its glass marble eyes shiny but empty. My dad has two stuffed deer heads in our basement. They are mounted on pieces of wood shaped like shields and I like to pet them when no one's watching, talk to them as if they're still alive.

Honeyboy still lives in Lemont Furnace, about twenty-five minutes from our house in Connellsville. Honeyboy doesn't work, and when I ask my mother about it, she says he's on disability because he has agoraphobia, which is an official way of saying he is afraid of being in public, around other people. He waits at home while his wife, Janette, goes into the hunting supply store. She buys several hunting jackets for Honeyboy, takes them home for him to try on. Then Janette goes back to the store and returns the ones that don't fit.

My dad started working at Anchor when he was eighteen, hitching a ride in the back of a neighbor's pickup truck five days a week. He's forty-seven years old now, has almost thirty years in, and is pretty high on the plant seniority list, a list that is the subject of much dinner table conversation between my parents, along with molds and plunger tests and union meetings.

Anchor only goes on shutdown two days a year: Christmas Eve and Christmas Day. On those days, a worker with high seniority can bid on a fire-watch shift. On a fire-watch shift, you simply hang around and check on the furnaces from time to time, making sure nothing ignites. Although no glass is being made, the furnaces can't be turned off, so someone needs to be there, sitting on a metal folding chair, watching. Workers are paid triple time for fire-watch shifts, so it's a very prestigious position in my mother's eyes, a position my father will be eligible for in a few years, once a few of the older men from The Hot End retire.

I've been inside the factory once, when they opened it up for tours in honor of their anniversary. My mother was recruited as a tour guide, and Linda and I got to be in her group. We all had to wear hairnets and foam earplugs and safety goggles to walk down the metal staircase that leads underground. At first I was worried about exposure to nuclear radiation because I'd seen the movie *Silkwood* with Cher and Meryl Streep on HBO one night, but my mother assured me it wasn't that kind of plant. Before the tour, I'd pictured the Anchor workers in white bodysuits, puffed up like astronauts. We'd been learning about NASA in IMPACT, the gifted program I'm enrolled in at school. We studied the parts of the space shuttle, and I became fascinated with the solid rocket boosters, the bright orange external tank, the orbiter, the only part that returns to Earth.

It's Saturday, March 16, 1985, and I wake up to the sound of bacon sizzling in the kitchen. Mother is off today, and she's making a big breakfast. Pancakes made with cornmeal instead of flour (her own special recipe—we call them corncakes) and extra-crispy bacon. Mother likes to cook before we wake up, so I never get to see the bacon transformation. Somehow it goes from long, flat, pink and white strips to brown hardened curls. They are snowflakes. No two are alike.

Linda is still sleeping. She's eleven years old, and a heavy sleeper. She doesn't normally wake up on weekends until noon, and she hates breakfast unless it's pancakes or French toast. "Go get your sister," Mother says, her right hand holding a pair of greased tongs.

I go into Linda's bedroom, where it's always dark, even in daylight. My bedroom is the opposite, the sheer curtains always letting the outside in. I pretend that her windowsill is a stage and pull open the drapes with their little rope and pulley system. I'm performing my version of *Annie,* my favorite movie. I have two different *Annie* albums—the original Broadway cast recording and the motion picture soundtrack. Both albums open up like a book to reveal color photo collages of all the characters.

"Act One: The Orphanage," I announce to the silent room, then break into my rendition of "Maybe." As the almost spring sunlight hits her face, Linda covers it with one pillow, then tries to throw the other one at my head. I finish my song and pull the curtain closed, and Linda rolls over, determined to go back to sleep. But the show isn't over yet. "Act Two: Miss Hannigan's Revenge," I say, followed by a spirited chorus of "It's the Hard Knock Life." Linda is not amused. She pulls herself out of bed, hugging her stuffed Pink Panther as she stumbles into the bathroom. I run down the hallway and back into the kitchen, where my mother is now juicing oranges. "Linda woke up all on her own," I report.

The dining room table is covered with a vinyl tablecloth, the kind that makes a *whooshing* sound when you wipe it down with a wet dishrag. The table is set for three. My father is still in bed. *The trouble* keeps him up at night. I hear him padding up and down the basement stairs throughout the night, the bathroom door closing with a soft click, a sliver of light shining through the crack above the floor. Linda emerges from the end of the hallway and sits down at the table. She begins pouring a river of maple syrup on her stack of corncakes.

Mother runs into the living room to turn off the stereo. She's been listening to 3WS, her oldies station, while she cooks, but she doesn't like music on while we eat. I think it would be fun to listen to the radio during a meal, and promise myself that when I grow up, my house will be wired with a sound system, speakers in every room, so I can listen to whatever I like whenever I like: Culture Club with breakfast, Olivia Newton-John with lunch, Michael Jackson with a midnight snack.

I have a system when it comes to corncakes, and there are multiple steps I must take before I can eat. First, I have to butter each cake and stack them one on top of the other. Then, I must cut them up into nine little squares with a knife and fork. Then, and only then, can I cover them in syrup. Linda is just the opposite, and it makes me nervous to watch her douse her corncakes in Log Cabin, then jab at them with her fork, stuffing misshaped bites into her mouth without counting. I'm finally getting around to taking my first bite when the telephone rings.

Mother goes into the kitchen, picks up the yellow trimline, and says hello. She listens for a minute or so, then bursts into a loud shrieklike noise, clapping a hand over her mouth with such force it sounds as though she's been slapped. Linda and I both stop mid-chew, curious but not alarmed. Mother is very dramatic when she's on the phone with her friends. One of my favorite pastimes is eavesdropping on her phone conversations. I usually sprawl out on the living room floor with a coloring book, listening to the one-sided conversation, playing the role of the caller inside my head. My mother talks like I'm not there. She swears and gossips and talks about people I don't know but I can imagine as if they're characters in some invisible play.

This call feels different. It actually feels like something bad has happened. I wonder if it's got something to do with Grandma Zelda.

My mother says Zelda's a hypochondriac, because she always thinks she's sick, even though she's healthy as a horse. Finally, my mother hangs up the phone. "There's been a shooting at Anchor," she says, nearly choking on the word *Anchor*. She bounds down the hall to wake Dad, and Linda and I sit there staring at our breakfast, unable to speak. There are moments that separate *before* from *after*, minutes in time that freeze like a photograph, capture a flash that indicates change. I start to realize that everything I've lived so far has been the *before*. I don't know what the *after* will be.

My mother is on the phone most of the morning, while my father decides to get out of bed and drive by the plant to check out the scene. I beg him to take me along, afraid he'll be shot if I'm not there to protect him, even though I'm not sure how I'll make my small body useful, become a child-size shield. I climb into the bucket seat on the passenger side of the Chevy Blazer, and we drive down Pittsburgh Street until it dead-ends at the factory gate. There are people milling around their parked cars in the gravel lot—men still wearing their dark coveralls, women still in hairnets and gloves. There are police cars, but no yellow tape wound around the trees like I imagined on the way over. There is no blood, no paramedics wheeling black body bags into an ambulance. The factory stacks look the same, billows of dark smoke streaming into the sky. My father doesn't stop to talk to anyone, just circles the parking lot slowly and then drives away.

Back at home, it takes hours and many conversations with different women for my mother to piece together what happened, but this is what she knows so far: A man named Sonny, who works in The Hot End, left his work area to talk to his wife, who works in The Cold End. One of the foremen saw him and called him into the office along with two other foremen and the plant manager. Sonny was suspended without pay for leaving his work area for personal business while not on a break. He was told he would have to file a grievance with the union and come back for a meeting next week. My parents are always talking about grievances, and my mother says there are certain employees who are grievance-crazy. "Some people will file a grievance if they don't like the way your shit smells in the bathroom," she says.

Sonny left Anchor after being suspended, and he went to the coffee shop at Pechin Shopping Village in Dunbar, where he ran into some other guys from work who were off today. Sonny told them about getting suspended, and the men spent a few minutes complaining about their bosses. Then Sonny said, "I should just go home and get my gun and shoot them." All the men laughed, but an hour later, Sonny walked into the factory and killed four supervisors before turning the gun on himself.

My mother says Sonny is a quiet man, like my father. He keeps his mouth shut and does his work. He doesn't get involved in plant politics. "He's just not one of the loud ones," she says. "Well, now I guess I should say he *wasn't* one of the loud ones." The expression on her face falls a bit, the corners of her mouth sagging, because she's realized she's talking about a dead person now. There's a certain way to talk about the dead, a certain feeling that must be observed, a remembrance.

My mother's cousin Vivian was at Anchor when it happened. She said because the factory floor was so noisy, a lot of workers didn't know what was going on. They could barely hear the gunshots. Glass started falling off the lines as workers ran for cover and machines jammed. The men in The Hot End had no idea, so they kept sending bottles and jars out to The Cold End, where glass began piling up on the floor, tumbling off the lines, smashing to the ground, piles of amber and green and flint everywhere. A group of women hid in the ladies' restroom and cried in panic.

When Sonny was finished killing people, he walked to the south end of the factory, to an area that smells like cardboard and grease—The Carton Department, they call it, where women pack bottles into cartons to ship off to the Rolling Rock Brewery or the Beech-Nut baby food plant. Sonny's wife ran up to him. She yelled something no one could understand. Sonny looked at her as he pointed the gun to his head, pulled the trigger. Some workers still didn't know what was going on as Sonny lay there in a pool of his own blood, his wife screaming.

The factory only closed until Sunday afternoon. When my mother returned to work the next day, men were there painting over trails of dried blood on the concrete floor, patching the hole in the foreman's office window with cardboard and duct tape. Everyone just went back to work. There was no meeting, no company memo, no explanation of what had happened, what went wrong. Sonny's wife was given three days off for bereavement, and then she was back to work, too. Connellsville made the evening news in Pittsburgh that night and a few days after. My father sat in the basement, staring at the TV while the newscaster read off the names of the men who died.

At school on Monday, as we complete our daily writing, Mrs. Swan kneels down beside my desk, strokes my long dark hair for a moment, and says, "I'm glad your parents are okay." Some of my classmates stare at me, as if they're waiting for my reaction, as if I have something to do with all of this.

I look up at the classroom ceiling and I can't see the lambs. The lions are orange and gold, their manes radiating out like sunbeams. They're taking up all the space in the room. Suddenly, I'm worried for my lamb. She's suspended from the ceiling with a paper clip and invisible fishing line. Her cotton wool hangs dangerously, the glue losing its stick. I smile at Mrs. Swan, say, "Thank you," and turn back to my work—those faint blue lines, that paper so coarse you can see the grain.

## CHAPTER 4

# Cross My Heart and Hope to Die

My parents knew Sonny, but they didn't know him well. They knew him in the way that they know everyone at Anchor. So many names are familiar, found on shop assignment postings and time cards, mentioned casually when we run into someone my mother knows, just the tossing out of a name as if it were light thrown against the air. We can't run errands around town without running into someone who knows my mother. On Fridays, Mellon Bank is a row of factory workers waiting to cash their checks, a receiving line of men and women waving hello to us or nodding in our direction as we take our place within the velvet ropes. People want to be close to my mother. She's a magnet, has a way of turning herself on when people are around. I like these moments, this turned-on version of my mother.

Other than Mellon Bank, downtown Connellsville has Troutman's department store, Mayer's Jewelry, McCrory's five and dime. There's the post office with two different mail slots—one for in-town mail and one for out-of-town mail. Once, when my mother sent me in alone to drop off the mail, I accidentally dropped an out-of-town letter through the in-town slot, and I gasped, my voice echoing through the chamber of the lobby, bouncing off the marble floors and sculpted ceiling. I got back in the car like nothing happened and then shut myself in the bathroom when we got home, letting the water run for a few minutes to muffle my sobbing.

There's also a tiny bakery, a blue and white storefront window where iced cakes perch on doilies on glass cake stands. It's called The Double B Bakery, owned by a very old couple. The woman walks permanently hunched over and uses a cane with a hook for a handle, like a giant candy cane. Linda has severe scoliosis, curvature of the spine, and when we see the little old woman leaving the shop with her ancient husband, my mother teases Linda. *You're going to look like that one day!* Linda's body is slightly crooked, and if you look at her closely you can see the slanted way she walks, the way one eye is slightly higher than the other. Her lips are straight, but behind them, her teeth and gums are sloping to one side.

She gets this from my father, who also has scoliosis, but in his childhood days nothing was done about it. Now, kids have to bend over and touch their toes in front of the school nurse while she feels your spine through your skin. After the school sent a note home about it, my parents took Linda to an orthopedic specialist in Uniontown, near the hospital where we were born. He recommended Linda wear a back brace, have surgery when her bones stop growing. He said it will likely get worse as she ages, and it doesn't help matters that she broke her collarbone when she was three years old. I was just a baby, only a few months old. Linda stood on one of the kitchen barstools to answer the telephone on the wall and she fell. At least that is how the story is told. I don't know why a three-year-old would answer the phone. I don't know what our parents were doing. My father is usually very careful about our movements—no cartwheels, no tumbling, no jumping from furniture.

My mother tells me Linda is the clumsy one and I'm the grace-ful one. Her words have a way of coming true, as if she can craft facts from her own ideas. My mother can think something and *poof,* it comes into being. She feels something and it is magically and swiftly transformed into fact. My mother believes acrobatics mess up a girl's insides, all that jumping and jarring, all that impact on your female parts. I never take acro at dance school, only tap, ballet, and jazz, even though I am desperate to do back handsprings and tinsi-cas, even though I want to walk on my hands more than anything, certain I would walk all over the house this way if I could, picking up things with my toes.

My classmates and teachers continue to ask me about Sonny, about the murderer. I understand their curiosity. I want to learn about him, too. The whole town is talking about this man now. Overnight he went from unknown factory worker to mass murderer. I know that what he did fits the definition of mass murder. Connellsville has a new celebrity, someone other than 1936 Olympic Gold Medalist Johnny Woodruff. People want to know about Sonny, about his wife, the two children he's left behind. I want to know what it was like when the children were told what their father did. I want to be a fly in that room, just a little bug on the ceiling, watching and listening. I'm very good at listening. Sometimes I'll press RECORD on the Sears tape recorder and then leave it where it can pick up my parents' voices, talking about work, talking "shop" as they say.

The factory is divided into different shops, but they are more like assembly lines, not actual storefronts. I picture an underground factory city my parents live in when they're not here. It's their home away from home and they are never there at the same time, only passing each other during shift change, the exchange of a glance, a key, a shopping list scribbled on the back of a work schedule.

Anyone is allowed to walk into the time card room, the only part of the factory that isn't underground. A man sits in a small guard booth behind a sliding-glass window. You have to get past him to make it down the staircase that leads in to the factory. Sonny pistol-whipped the guard on duty the day of the shooting, left him slumped over the tiny counter of his booth, bleeding. Now, in the aftermath of the shooting, there are hired armed guards at the entrance of the plant. No one is sure how long they will stay.

Workers' kids are allowed in the time card room. We're allowed to examine the metal slats filled with card stock (oak tag, Mrs. Swan calls it—that stiff beige paper we use when construction paper is too flimsy, too weak to hold up our ideas). Each worker has a clock number and my parents know each other's by heart. My father plays the Pennsylvania Lottery with them regularly, and he won The Daily Number drawing once with his clock number—634.

My father and Linda and I were in the basement, watching the evening news. The drawing comes right after, and it's exciting to watch it live—to watch the numbered Ping-Pong balls float up three tubes until the winning combination of numbers appears. One digit at a time, the suspense builds. My father keeps his stack of lottery tickets on the end table, flips through them to find the right one for the occasion. He's got his thumb on the numbers, and Linda and I are on our feet, rooting for the right ones to be called. I'm rooting for champagne wishes and caviar dreams from my mother's favorite program—*Lifestyles of the Rich and Famous.* I'm rooting for a yacht, its impractical stern floating somewhere in the Yough as we leave town.

The first number is called, and it's a match, but this has happened before. We've been disappointed by numbers too often to get excited now. The second number is called and it's also a match. My father stands up from his recliner, then gets down on one knee, looking into the eye of the television like it's a camera lens about to snap his picture and he is posing. Linda and I are jumping up and down.

We're little girls, jumping up and down is what we do best. The third number is called and it's a match. We've won. It still feels impossible, but we've won. My father, still on one knee, clutches the ticket even tighter, dramatically falls onto his side, pretending to faint.

He's won $600, which isn't exactly a jackpot, but it feels like a victory. It feels like I've been holding something up for a long time and I can finally let it go, even if only for a minute. My shoulders relax and I wish my parents owned wineglasses or champagne flutes, something we could use for a fake toast. But then I remember that it's bad luck to toast with water, so I'm glad.

★ ★ ★

I have rituals for reaching the dew point. First, I have to be under a blanket. In my bedroom, that's easy. I can do it at bedtime all I want, even though I must be quiet because all of our bedroom doors remain open while we sleep. My room, Linda's room, and my parents' room are all lined up at the end of the long hallway. Ours is a brick ranch house, built in the early 1970s. It's got a long hallway with one bathroom, powder blue, and the three bedrooms nestled side by side. My bedroom is the smallest and warmest of the three. The furnace room is directly beneath me when I sleep, a room of four concrete walls my father painted red. It scares me, reminds me of reading Truman Capote's *In Cold Blood*, a true crime novel the old librarian let me check out from the Carnegie downtown. One of the members of the Clutter family was found dead in their furnace room, gagged and bound to a dining room chair.

I don't have to be in my room to reach the dew point. I can do it on the couch in the basement while we're all watching TV or my dad is behind an unfolded newspaper, reading. My mother crocheted a lot while pregnant in the '70s. She only knew how to make afghans, and only in one pattern—the zigzag two-color pattern that looks like the design on Charlie Brown's shirt. Our basement is decorated in all sorts of dark and neutral jewel tones—topaz, garnet, amber. The carpet looks like tiny panels of stained glass in these colors. Some walls are painted bright orange while others are covered in dark wood paneling. The afghans were designed to match. One is yellow and green, one is brown and orange, another is cream and brown. They are soft from many washings and live folded up on the back of the couch.

I'll lay down and pretend to watch TV, cover myself in an afghan, and slowly slide my left hand inside my pants. Sometimes I'll rub through my underwear, and sometimes I'll go for skin to skin—my fingers against my folds. I have to do it slowly when my dad and Linda are around. Too quick and my body makes noises I don't want them to hear.

One evening, I go up to my bedroom early so I can reach the dew point. No one ever goes to bed before ten o'clock in this house. I shouldn't be so conspicuous, but I can't help myself. I am rubbing myself, just staring straight up at the ceiling. The ceilings in our house have texture, semicircles that fan and swoop as if the builder combed through the plaster before it dried. When they poured our new sidewalk, I saw the men from Stone & Co. use what looked like rakes and brooms. They were marking the sidewalk plates, making neat little raised rows that will eventually fade, be stomped out by the mailman, by neighbor kids walking home from school in the afternoon. Linda and I were allowed to write our initials in the wet cement at one end of our sidewalk, right next to where our sidewalk ends and our neighbor's sidewalk begins. We also got to place two pennies next to our initials—1984 pennies, heads-up, brand new from the bank. My mother asked for them specifically, wanted coins that hadn't been circulated yet. Eventually someone will pick both pennies out of the dried cement, but I don't know that yet. I think that money will always be there. My father said it was me and Linda giving the house our two cents. I imagine us as the only little girls that will ever live here, the only girl bodies that will ever lay down in the blue bathtub.

I'm about to reach the dew point when my mother comes in to my room, flips on the light. She pulls the covers off my bed and I'm just there with my hand in my white panties.

"Open the goddamn window!" she yells. "It smells like your god-damn ass in here!" She's leaning over me, she's biting her tongue in between words. It's something I do, too, when I feel something strong, something I can't get out with words or my hands. I recognize myself in her and that scares me. I stand up and run to the corner of the room, place myself there the way teachers put bad kids like Jimmy Carter in little invisible cells. If you turn around, you have to stay in the corner even longer. But I'm putting myself here. I know how to punish myself. I look down and notice a spot of blood on the front of my underwear. Did I rub myself too hard?

"Now I have to wash these goddamned sheets!" my mother screams. Linda and my father are downstairs watching TV and eating microwave popcorn. I want to get down there, would give anything for a secret passageway leading from my bedroom closet to the basement, like the trap doors in the game of Clue.

"But I wasn't doing anything," I hear myself whisper. I didn't mean to say it out loud.

"Liar!" my mother yells.

I think I'll just make a run for it, even though I'm half naked. I could always stop in the laundry room on the way down the hall, just grab a dirty nightgown, anything to cover me up until I make it to the brown couch and wrap myself in an afghan. But my mother isn't letting me out of this room. I make a move to the right and she's right there, so close to my face I can see the finger marks of blush on her cheeks. I'm crying now, I don't even know why. I don't know what I think she'll do to me. She's never hit me before with her hands. She hits with her words, syllables like pellets popping from a gun.

"I want to get Dad," I tell her. "Please just let me go get Dad." I'm pleading, not just because I'm afraid for myself, but also because I think Mom needs some kind of help. She needs another adult in this room. Something's wrong, some kind of switch has been tripped, some sort of activation. Is this what happens when someone breaks and starts hurting people? I picture Sonny biting his tongue each time he squeezes the trigger. I picture Sonny making his victims stand in corners.

One of the stories that came out after the shooting is that one of the foremen working that day hid behind the door when Sonny came into his office to kill him. The man could hear Sonny reloading his gun on the other side of the door. This foreman was so scared he started peeing his pants. He was worried that Sonny would see the stream of piss leading out from under the door, but this guy was fortunate. Maybe he'd picked up a four-leaf clover that day. Or maybe he carried a rabbit's foot in his pocket. Sonny didn't notice the foreman behind the door, he just went on his way, killing one more person, then himself.

I wish there was a door between my mother and me right now, something I could hide behind until she passes, but I'm not so lucky. She grabs me by my bare shoulders, throws me onto the stripped-down mattress.

I land on my back with a bounce and my mother's on top of me—crying and yelling in my face, but I can't make out the words, can only feel the heat of her anger like a cloud heavy with rain hovering above us, like my bedroom ceiling is a sky. I just want her to hit me, to get it over with. The sting of her hand on my face feels like an ending, and I welcome it. When she collapses to the floor, I jump up and stand on the bed. It's hard to walk over the springs of the mattress, but I do, and they creak under my feet. If this were a cartoon, every step would make a *boing* sound, exaggerated and loud.

I grab a nightgown from the chest of drawers. My mother says little girls don't wear pajamas, they wear silky nightgowns with no panties underneath. I dress quickly and step over my mother's body. She's on the floor within the tangle of bed sheets and pillows. She yells after me, "Don't you dare tell your father about this!" and I let her words echo down the hallway as I try to walk instead of run.

## CHAPTER 5

# Stick a Needle in My Eye

My mother must think I'm beautiful, because she's entered me in a beauty pageant for little girls. A woman from the factory named Shirley Abel makes a party dress for me to wear, turquoise taffeta under white eyelet. The word taffeta reminds me of taffy, the fabric stiff and shiny in my hands. My mother takes me to Shirley's house for measurements. Shirley lives alone now, her two sons grown and married with kids of their own. Her husband, Bill, was one of the foremen Sonny killed at the factory. Bill was one of the nice ones, too, according to my mother. "Sonny didn't even get the right bastards," she says. I wonder who the right bastards are. Who are the people who deserve to die? Before the shooting, I didn't think anyone in our town deserved it, but I'm beginning to change my mind.

With a soft blue roll of numbered tape, Shirley measures my hips and waist, the lengths of my arms, and my girth, which is my least favorite part because it involves stretching the tape from my crotch to one shoulder, crossing my chest like Linda's Girl Scout sash, the one I like to look at when Linda's sleeping, sneaking into her room to touch the embroidered triangles, the troop number, the small gold stars that must represent something.

The pageant is held at the Hilton in Pittsburgh, the hotel where Elvis stayed back in 1976, when he played a concert in the city, on tour before he died the next year. My mother and father went to the show, me in fetus form peering out to watch through my mother's belly button, or at least that's how the story is told.

I have a different outfit for every part of the pageant. I wear a white cotton jumper with rainbow-colored hearts for the arrival activities, which include being photographed with the woman who founded the pageant. She has slick red fingernails, and hair smoothed into a Dorothy Hamill flip, like a mushroom cap over her scalp. I wear a pink and white pinstriped seersucker short suit for the sportswear competition, a pastel pink clip-on necktie, and ruffled ankle socks. For the ice-cream social, where a clown makes balloon animals for all the contestants, I wear a burgundy Christian Dior pinafore dress, with white tights and black patent leather Mary Janes.

My mother gives me a new hairstyle to match each outfit. Between each change, my hair is watered, sprayed, wrapped in sponge curlers, ironed, teased, parted, oiled like machinery, fitted with barrettes and ribbons and bobby pins. I chew gum while my mother does her work, and my father and Linda play 500 Rum on the hotel room table, cruise the gift shop for candy and magazines.

The highlight of the competition arrives toward the end of the day. It's nine o'clock in the evening, and the girls are showing signs of unrest. We slump ourselves in chairs backstage while mothers shove our small feet into shoes black as licorice. We spread out on the floor, lying on newspapers our mothers provide so we won't soil our dresses, which ruffle and shine and unfurl when we finally stand. We're getting ready for the beauty portion of the pageant, and we will be judged on how beautiful we look in our dresses, how neat and well-groomed our mothers have made our hair, how clearly we speak when the host asks us each one question.

I am tall for my age, so I must stand in the back row of the risers, on the stage with no curtain, no red velvet veil to raise and lower between each act, no stagehand in the wings pulling a rope to reveal fifty little girls wearing eye shadow and their mothers' jewelry. I am the second to last girl to make her way down to the announcer, to talk into the dented microphone, its cord snaking around the stage like a thin garden hose I must step over carefully. The announcer wants to know what I want to be when I grow up. He asks me in an official announcer voice, which makes my answer feel official, as if it will be carved into stone after I speak.

I haven't been listening to the other girls' responses. I've been staring into a stage light at the edge of the riser, inspecting the blue film that's been placed over it. It reminds me of a project we completed in IMPACT, the gifted program I go to once a week. It's a program for kids with IQs above 135. We had to make our own light of some sort, had to learn how to connect the black and red wires, the positive and negative lines that make a lightbulb burn when you screw it in. I made a stoplight out of a shoebox, cut three holes in the cardboard, and painted it black. I placed a lightbulb in each hole, stretched a colored film across each smooth circle—green, yellow, red. I programmed it to light in sequence like a real traffic light. Steady green, brief yellow, steady red.

Now I'm standing with the announcer, who's on one knee as if he wants to marry the girls, wants to come down to our level so he can see our faces. I can't think of an answer the judges may want to hear, so I say I want to be a secretary, even though that is probably the one career option I've never written down in the "School Days" scrapbook my mother keeps, two pages for each year.

I don't win anything except a small trophy they give out for participation. "That's one expensive trophy," my mother says as she melts into the front seat of the Lincoln on the way home to Connellsville. My father doesn't respond, my mother's words just hanging in the air until no one is sure what she just said. We pass Point State Park, the famous fountain spraying water that is bright white with light. I see boats along the river at Station Square, the reflection of everything on the water, rivers everywhere in this city.

After we pass through the Squirrel Hill Tunnels, my mother tells a story. It's the story of what I should have said, and it goes like this. "You should have said you wanted to be a meteorologist. The announcer would have chuckled, amazed by how smart you are, and he would have asked you what a meteorologist is, to which you would have replied *the weather girl on TV!* You would have won the pageant with that answer. You would have won."

Amy Nickels is my best friend, and she's a tomboy, so she thinks my pageant career is weird. And it is. I'm not sure what my mother thinks I'll gain from all this. I don't think I'll ever be much of a winner in these competitions. The girls who win seem to be smaller than me, more compact. My limbs look like tree trunks next to their branches. And I look older, too. They still have their milk teeth, straight and small and white. I'm shedding baby teeth everywhere it seems, always wiggling something in my mouth. I hate to pull them out myself and prefer to wait until my teeth are hanging by a string of gum or they fall out on their own. It's disgusting, according to my mother, and if I let her see inside my mouth, she'll reach in and grab one, twist it out in seconds, throw it into a Dixie cup.

My mother is rough with me. She combs out my long wet hair after a bath, tugging and pulling until my scalp is sore to the touch. When it's a particularly hard case, she'll get out the electric comb, a dark blue device with large white teeth bigger than tines on a fork. She'll work it back and forth through my hair until I cry, but it's my fault for not brushing my hair more. One hundred strokes a night is her prescription for me, but my arms get tired after thirty or so. I watched *Mommie Dearest* on HBO and saw myself in the scene where Christina Crawford is sitting at her mother's vanity, pretending to accept an award in the mirror, a golden brush as her microphone. Her mother, Joan Crawford, played by Faye Dunaway, who is usually beautiful, but scary as this character with her razor-thin painted eyebrows and pale made-up skin, catches her playacting and thinks she's being arrogant, ungrateful.

Joan starts to comb the curls out of Christina's hair, but the little girl has used her mother's setting lotion, and the hair simply won't move through the brush. Joan pulls and tugs at the girl's curls, the girl's scalp on fire, the girl wailing, in tears, until finally her mommie dearest takes out the scissors and starts chopping away at her pretty blond curls. Mommie dearest is teaching Christina a lesson without words. Even a child can recognize that. There can only be one star in any house. There's not enough light for two. That's the lesson, little girl. That's all you need to know.

# CHAPTER 6

# Eat Well, You Hound

"It's not a sin to be poor, but it *is* a sin to be dirty." My mother's eyes nearly glow in the dimly lit bedroom as she states this belief, first held by my dead grandmother, then my mother, and now, presumably, me. My mother folds towels while she talks. I sit cross-legged on her yellow and green bedspread, watching her. She has this trifold technique and works too quickly for me to figure out the moves. I stare at stacks of perfectly folded blue towels in the bathroom closet and then unfold one carefully, making mental notes, yet somehow I can never get it back to the way it was.

"What if the poor people can't afford soap?" I ask. "Is it still a sin?"

"Listen carefully," she says, clearly exhausted by me. "Some people may not choose to be poor, but they *do* choose to be dirty."

My mother cleans a lot. Many days I return home from school to find her on her hands and knees with a bucket of bleach water, wiping down the baseboards, fumes burning my nose hairs if I get too close to her. My mother is forty-four years old and has already lost her sense of smell from nearly twenty-three years of working at Anchor, where she inhales glass furnace exhaust and asbestos residue.

My mother can't do laundry, or iron, or wash dishes on Sundays. She can make dinner, as long as she only uses the stovetop burners, not the oven. Using your oven on Sunday is strictly forbidden and brings bad luck. You can't even open the oven door, unless you want something bad to happen.

Once, when Linda needed her Brownie uniform cleaned on a Sunday evening, my mother refused to so much as show her how to turn on the washing machine. "That would constitute work, and I don't work on the Sabbath," she explained. Linda stood on a chair, baffled by the buttons and dials on the cream-colored Maytag.

"But you work at the factory on Sundays all the time," I remind her.

"That's different because I don't have a choice in the matter. But I do have a choice when it comes to housework." She lingers in the doorway for a moment, holding a cup of instant coffee in her hands as if to warm her fingers, which are bony and always cold. Dad expects Mother has ruined most of the nerve endings in her fingers from handling hot bottles with her bare hands when she was younger.

"She never did like the way those bulky red gloves looked on her," he tells me when I ask how Mother can wash her hands with water so hot it fogs the bathroom mirror with a coat of steam. "You better not use the faucet right after her unless you don't mind getting scalded," he warns me. "Best to let the pipes cool first."

My mother acts as though it is her personal mission in life to clean the world—to rid it of dirt, dust, mildew, unwashed hair, dingy windows, soiled carpets, rusted cars on blocks in overgrown back-yards. She warns me not to befriend the dirty kids in school, the ones labeled as "scurfs" in local kid language. The Murphy family is the most famous scurf family in town. There are so many of them, one in practically every grade at South Side Elementary. You can hear the taunts on the playground, on the steps leading up to the blond brick school, the glass double doors, *Scurfy Murphy*. Anyone can be a scurfy Murphy, the highest form of verbal punishment a kid can dish out.

There are so many poor families in Connellsville, home to abandoned coke ovens, pizza parlors, bars, and churches. There are so many half-crumbling houses with tar paper roofs, so many kids living in the housing project by the high school stadium, so many welfare bums as my mother calls them. They seem to be just like me. Many of them are smart, make good grades in school, even though they smell like old food, or cigarette smoke, or urine. Even though Amy Nickels is one of them, and even though I'm hiding it from my mother, she is becoming my best friend.

Amy is hilarious. One of our favorite rituals is analyzing skits from *Saturday Night Live* on Monday mornings. We have the same sense of humor. We're *precocious,* according to Amy's mother. Her name is Bubbles and she is twenty years younger than my mother, with beautiful red hair down her back. I look precocious up in the dictionary. When referring to a child, precocious means *having developed certain abilities or proclivities at an earlier age than usual.* The word can also refer to a plant *flowering or fruiting earlier than usual.*

Amy can write and draw really well, and she loves comic books. Once, she wrote and illustrated a comic book called "Mr. Smarty Pants and the Jumpy Toupee." Mr. Smarty Pants is a man whose pants have been enchanted by a sea-witch, so they come to life and talk. They are always ruining the day. When Mr. Smarty Pants is at work giving an important presentation in front of his bosses, his pants decide to unzip themselves and fall down around his ankles, exposing his boxer shorts, which are covered in little pink hearts. Mr. Smarty Pants' toupee is also possessed, jumping off his head at the worst possible times.

Amy is in IMPACT with me, so every Thursday we are shipped to another elementary school in a van so we can learn how to program computers and make various things out of papier-mâché and plaster of Paris. Our second-grade classmates call our IMPACT trips "nerd conventions." When we study dinosaurs, I set out to construct a model Tyrannosaurus rex, but I don't hold his head up long enough while he dries, so he ends up looking more like a brontosaurus. I give him a smiley face instead of a snarl to try to cover up my mistake.

When we study Egypt, I make a tiny sarcophagus out of Popsicle sticks, which I spray-paint gold. Inside is a little King Tut, his body molded from clay, then covered in plaster of Paris, like a real mummy. If you crack him open, you'll see he has arms and legs and everything, as I used a sharp toothpick to carve them out of the soft green clay. He's also wearing his famous mask, the one with the blue and gold stripes and the serpent between his eyes. I keep King Tut in my bedroom, take him out of his little coffin every night, cup his still body in the palm of my hand the way I imagine a mother might.

I want Amy to be interested in murders and other tragedies, but they seem to roll down her back, spilling over her yellow hair. I'll try to strike up a conversation about the made-for-TV movie I saw last night, *Fatal Vision,* about a man who killed his pregnant wife and two daughters, then claimed it was a group of Manson family copycats. He stabbed his wife with an ice pick, bludgeoned and stabbed the girls to death, then wrote "pig" on a headboard in their blood. He was an army doctor, so he knew how to pull off a self-inflicted stabbing. To make it look like he was attacked without really hurting himself. He knew the map of veins and arteries in the torso, knew exactly where to cut. A superficial wound it's called. I look up superficial in the dictionary. In this context, it means *situated or occurring on the skin or immediately beneath it.* It has other meanings, too. I think one of them could be used to describe my mother: *not having or showing any depth of character or understanding.* My mother is always quoting Zsa Zsa Gabor, mimicking her thick Hungarian accent. *Dahling, if you can't look your best, you shouldn't even leave the house!* There's another definition for this entry: *appearing to be true or real only until examined more closely.* I'm beginning to notice many things that appear real until you get closer. My mother's false eyelashes, the plastic log in our decorative fireplace in the basement. It actually plugs into the wall, and you can flip a switch and make it glow red from within. It even makes a fake crackling noise.

Some things aren't real, but we think we see them, like a mirage, water appearing to a thirsty person in the desert. Can our minds really play tricks on us? Make us see things that aren't even there?

My father is going back to work and I'm worried for him. His first shift back is the night shift, the worst one of all. Even though he's not a foreman, I'm afraid of angry men shooting him overnight with guns they pull from inside their dark overalls, foremen who don't like the way he moves. What will they do to him when he returns to the furnaces, The Hot End floor, all that overheated cement? My mother says everyone at the factory knows that my father's been on sick leave for his nerves, and I'm sure this is true. I've heard her spreading the news as she leans over the orange kitchen countertop, the phone cradled between her shoulder and chin. The telephone lines in a small town like ours burn with gossip, a constant stream of discussion that is simply a way of life around here.

I'm afraid people will tease my father for being nervous. The doctors in Pittsburgh never found anything wrong with him, no diagnosis, no disease, but his sick leave is running out and my mother is complaining about the Discover Card bill, how the balance keeps growing and needs to be paid. Before the many different test results came in, after getting enemas and colonoscopies and swallowing tubes and taking needles in the creases of his arms, I worried about cancer in my father's bowels, imagined tumors growing dark and thick in his body, a wild black stalk of something, an uninvited guest taking over. But it's not cancer, not now.

We take my father to Anchor to drop him off for his first day back to work. My mother is driving the Lincoln, dad on the passenger side. Linda and I are in the backseat, our bare feet brushing the scratchy red carpet of the floor mats. At shift change, there is a line along the curb, a slow procession of men and women getting into and out of cars and trucks, saying hello, saying goodbye. My mother parks and I lean forward to whisper in her ear. "Is that mean supervisor going to be there today? The one who said *I don't like the way you move?*" I want to know whether he's one of the dead men, one of Sonny's victims, or if he's one of the lucky bastards who got away.

My mother is angry now. She pushes my face away, shouts at me to sit down. I don't know if it's my question that's made her so mad or the fact that I've gotten too close to her face. She seems to live within a layer of glass, like a snow globe nobody can enter, especially little girls.

The four of us sit in silence for a minute or two, watching people file in and out of the factory gate. I look over at Linda and she appears to be blank, like the smooth tiles in Scrabble that don't have letters on them. She is wiped clean. Just sitting there in the backseat of this big car, staring out the window and picking at her thumbs, a bad habit my mother scolds her for. Linda picks her thumbs raw, bloody scabs all around her thumbnails that bloom all the way down to her knuckles. When it gets bad enough, my mother wraps two flesh-colored Band-Aids around the thumb—one over the top of the thumb like a hat, and one that wraps around the thumb knuckle like a belt. Linda's thumbs are little people under those bandages, trying to grow new skin like new faces. But as soon as the bandages come off, she digs the skin open again, breaks it apart, pink and wet and new.

That night while my father works, Linda and I crawl into bed with our mother. Linda is on my father's side of the bed, closest to the nightstand, the clock radio with its white needle, the little jar of rose salve for his cracked hands. I lay in the middle of the bed sucking my thumb, the left one tonight. I've decided that the left one is cherry flavor and the right one is lemon flavor, and cherry is my favorite. Linda is picking her thumb and I'm sucking mine and our mother is already sleeping, her blond head sunk into the pillow, her back facing me, always facing me. When I wake up, my thumb will be white and shriveled, small bits of the skin shredding, my teeth sore. While we sleep our father moves slowly around a furnace, sweats over glass, while we do what we can to break ourselves open, still breaking, always breaking.

# CHAPTER 7

# May You Be Sick and I Be Sound

I'm afraid of the dark. When I walk through the house at night, I flip on every light along my way. I can't watch horror movies the way Amy and her brothers do. They love the *Friday the 13th* movies and *A Nightmare on Elm Street*. They laugh at the fake blood and guts, Freddy Krueger's leather glove, his razor-blade fingers. It's just corn syrup, Amy tells me, it's just a prop, but it doesn't matter. I know it's fiction, that the images aren't real. That's not the problem. The problem is that the things in the movies could happen. Every scene represents some kind of evil that could exist. Scary movies are tempting fate. They're tempting possibility. Anything is possible. I know that. Just because you've never seen something doesn't mean it doesn't exist.

I had nightmares for two weeks after Linda dared me to watch Michael Jackson's "Thriller" video on MTV. After it was over, I went to the bathroom, and she waited quietly outside the door until I was done, then jumped out and scared me when I opened it. I screamed and fell to my knees. She made me promise I wouldn't tell our mother.

Amy doesn't want to act out scenes from *Fatal Vision* with me. We could play the dead daughters, lying on the floor in pools of our own blood. But who would play the killer, Amy asks? She doesn't want to pretend to die from leukemia either, thinks it's strange when I act out the final scene from a movie I watched about a little girl with cystic fibrosis who only lives to be eight years old. In the movie she dies propped up in her little girl bed, pillows and stuffed animals and ruffles around her face.

I'm too healthy, and I think about what it would be like if I had a disease. I watch the commercials for St. Jude's Research Hospital, the kids with their smooth hairless heads, their smiles, surrounded by mounds of greeting cards in their hospital rooms. I wouldn't mind receiving that kind of attention. Maybe my mother would feel bad about being mean to me then. Maybe she would see my sickness as punishment for her cruelty. She'd beg and plead to the sky, to the stars, *just make Karen well and I promise I'll be better!* The kids at school would feel horrible, too.

Julie Walls would cry and pray for me to be okay, and she'd feel sorry for teasing me about my hairy legs and arms. Sitting next to me in reading group last year, in first grade, she made up a song, kept whispering it in my ear, cupping her mouth with her hand as if we were sharing a secret: *hairy hairy hairy legs, hairy hairy hairy arms.*

Julie's mother is named Edie. She's my mother's age. They were kids at the same time in South Connellsville, playing on the monkey bars together. One night as it started getting dark and they both walked to their houses, Edie complained to my mother that her legs hurt. The next morning, when Edie woke up, she couldn't get out of bed. She'd contracted polio. The year was 1951 and my mother and Edie were ten years old. Jonas Salk was at the University of Pittsburgh, only fifty-seven miles away from us, developing the polio vaccine. It would be officially announced to the public in 1955, but that would be too late for Edie. She has been in a wheelchair ever since, and because she played on a rusty set of monkey bars, my mother doesn't want me or Linda going anywhere near them. Maybe Julie is mean because her mother is in a wheelchair and that makes her mad at the world. I understand that, really I do. I just don't understand what that has to do with me and my hairy arms and legs. I don't understand why I'm here, other than to be the girl others use when they need someone to scare, someone to blame, someone to hurt.

We have a small playground just a block down the street from our house. Most kids in the neighborhood hang out there after school, and all day long in the summer. When we drive by in the Lincoln, on our way to Warehouse Groceries or Uniontown Mall, I'll look out the window and see girls on the seesaw, boys on the swings, daring each other to see how high they can go, jumping off at the highest point, sticking the landing the way a gymnast does at the Olympics. My mother says she knows that polio is a viral infection, but isn't it a coincidence that Edie fell ill right after she played on those rusty bars? There must be a connection. Some things, according to my mother, can't be explained by science. Sometimes you just feel the answers. And even though you have no way of proving it, you just know it's the truth.

★ ★ ★

Linda and I are in the shower together, in a hotel room somewhere in North Carolina. We're practicing our tap routines, our bare feet splashing water out of the tub, soaking our clothes, which are crumpled on the floor beyond the frosty shower curtain. We're on our way to Orlando, Florida. We're going to Walt Disney World, and I'm going to get my picture taken with Mickey Mouse, but for now, we've stopped here at a Days Inn for the night.

There's only a month left of second grade, and I get to miss an entire week for the trip, promising Mrs. Swan I'll bring her back a souvenir, something Florida-ish, a starfish or a seashell. Dad drove the four of us here from Pennsylvania in the Chevy Blazer, Linda and I sprawled out on the bench seat in the back, eating Hostess cupcakes and practicing spelling-bee words from Linda's practice book. "Loquacious," I say somewhere in West Virginia.

"That's easy," Linda says. "L-o-q-u-a-c-i-o-u-s."

"You forgot to say the word before and after you spell it," I remind her. "And remember, you can always ask for the definition or part of speech." I love the rules of competitive spelling, how rigid they are: the judges and their emotionless faces, the little bell they ring when a speller is eliminated. There are no second chances in the spelling-bee world. One mistake and you're off the stage. You're history.

Linda and I know we are too old to shower together, but my mother wants us to get ready for bed as quickly as possible. So we splash around a little longer, emptying the tiny hotel-size conditioner into our long hair, then turn the water off and wrap ourselves in the thin white towels the hotel staff has provided.

Outside the bathroom door, my mother is sobbing to my father, but I can't make out the words. All day, she's been unhappy about something. She didn't want to drive in the first place. She wanted to take an airplane to Florida, like we did last year when we took a trip to Fort Myers Beach. My mother planned that entire vacation through a Sears travel agent—flight, rental car (a Lincoln Town Car), hotel on the beach, even a day trip on a fishing boat where Linda and I caught nothing but blowfish. Their bloated bodies looked brittle, as if they were made from paper. I'd reel in my line and scream when I saw one hanging there, its spines dripping with water from the Gulf of Mexico.

This year's trip, to Disney World, was my father's idea. He didn't go though the travel agent at Sears in the Uniontown Mall. He booked everything on his own. So far, my mother hasn't approved of one thing about this trip. Right now, she's sobbing because our motel room is on the corner of the hotel complex, close to the Dumpster.

When Linda and I come out of the bathroom in our nightgowns, our towels now fashioned into makeshift turbans, Mother is rocking back and forth on the edge of one of the double beds, the floral bedspread a horrible mix of burgundy and green.

"I just feel doomed here, next to the trash. It's scary. We could be murdered in our sleep, our bodies thrown in the Dumpster," she says. "It could be days before they find us!" she screams, then marches into the still humid bathroom, closing the door with a slam behind her. Linda and I glance at each other, but we don't speak. Linda sits down on the bed and starts studying her spelling words, while I find my Rainbow Brite doll, fussing with the few strands of bright orange hair that have escaped from her ponytail.

My father picks up the phone, dials the front desk. He requests another room, goes to the lobby to trade the keys. Mother emerges from the bathroom with mascara smudged all over her face. She is silent. Dad and Linda and I lug all of our stuff into the new hotel room, which smells like an air-conditioned ashtray. Mother peels back the scratchy bedspread on one of the beds, lies down, and closes her eyes.

We've been to Disney World once, in 1980, but I was only three years old, so I don't remember the trip. I've seen pictures of Linda and me sitting on a beach wearing matching souvenir T-shirts. They are bright yellow with smiling oranges on them. The lettering says FRESH-SQUEEZED FROM FLORIDA! as if the oranges are more than happy to be turned into juice. My hair is parted down the middle, two thick braids hanging to my waist.

On that trip back in 1980, there was a caravan of us making the drive. My grandfather, JR, was still alive and he financed the entire thing. Pam and her first husband were just married, and they followed us in their Caprice. Then Uncle Roger and his wife, Joanie, followed in their car. JR rode with them so he could smoke the whole way down. We stopped at South of the Border, that famous tourist attraction off I-95. It's modeled after a Mexican village. My mother bought a scarf there, pictures of tiny cactuses and sombreros all over it. My father bought Linda a pair of castanets, me a set of maracas. We must have made our own little band in the vinyl backseat of the car.

My mother says that JR knew he would die soon, and he wanted to do something fun with his remaining son and daughter and their families, but the trip seemed to be plagued by bad luck. First, Pam's husband lost his turnpike ticket in the crack between the car's windshield and dashboard, so they had to pay the highest fare when they arrived at the tollbooth. Then, after a few days in the Florida sun, Pam got a sunburn so severe she could barely move, wrapping herself in a soaking wet towel under an umbrella the rest of the week. Then Uncle Roger and his wife, Joanie, stole all the towels and bedspreads from the hotel in Kissimmee and my grandfather was humiliated at the front desk, the clerk threatening to call the police if he didn't pay for the damages.

I don't remember any of these things. I've only heard these stories from my mother, so the trip remains a shiny memory in my mind. There's another picture of the whole group of us standing in the breezeway just outside our hotel rooms. It's a Polaroid and has that hazy look that I've come to associate with the 1970s, a decade I was born in, yet have no concrete memories of. In silent home movies from when I was a baby, my mother and Pam wore bell-bottom jeans and floppy hats. We didn't have our in-ground pool back then, and no fancy landscaping in the backyard. Instead, there was a blue inflatable baby pool and lots of grass to roll around on. There was a driveway made of gravel, and Linda and I used to throw the stones at the fence just for fun, or at least that's what I've seen in the home movies.

My mother doesn't like being photographed unless she's posing, and my father likes nothing more than to snap candid photographs of her. This has resulted in many reels of film consisting of my father sneaking up on my mother and surprising her with the camera. She always puts her hands up to the lens like a movie star shooing away photographers. Finally, she fixes her hair for a second, then smiles, turning away when she's decided Dad has had enough.

This new trip to Disney in 1985 is different—but still haunted with bad luck. I think the worst part of it all is that I'll be old enough to remember it this time.

On the second day of our trip, we drive from somewhere in North Carolina all the way to our hotel near Disney World. It's a long day, my mother sitting motionless in the passenger seat, my father trying to keep things light by playing memory games with me and Linda like The Picnic Game, a game where we take turns listing items we'd take to a picnic, trying to remember what the other players have said. You begin your turn by saying *I'm going on a picnic and I'm going to take* . . . and you fill in the blank with something that starts with the first letter of your first name. The game ends when someone can't remember the list of items or when someone can't think of any more picnic items beginning with the first letter of their first name.

These games are hard for me because there aren't many words that begin with *k,* and I've already used Kool-Aid, kangaroo, and kaleidoscope. Bringing a kangaroo to a picnic is a bit of a stretch, but my dad and Linda allow it.

My mother can't be bothered with having a good time on this trip. On the days we're not at the park, she's in the hotel bed while the rest of us go swimming and miniature golfing and out for ice cream. Of the three days we're scheduled for visits to the Disney parks, we'll spend two at Magic Kingdom and one at EPCOT, which is the newest addition to the park. It's an acronym that stands for Experimental Prototype Community of Tomorrow, and while I'm there I believe I'm the happiest I've ever been in my life.

I fall in love with the *Journey Into Imagination* ride, the small purple-winged dragon named Figment projected into the darkness as we roll along in small pods. I want to ride it a second time, but my father isn't sure we'll have time to wait in the line again before the night ends. It's our last day at Disney, and I'm afraid I'll never get to see Figment again. In the gift shop, my father buys me a small stuffed version of Figment. He wears a yellow and red T-shirt with his name on it.

Yellow and red are my two favorite colors. Amy knows this. For my last birthday she wrote *Happy Birthday, Karen* inside my card with red and yellow markers, alternating colors with every letter. When I opened the card, I was embarrassed to find out she cared about me enough to do that. I didn't know how else to feel. I could tell Amy was waiting for me to say something about the gesture, but I couldn't. I opened my mouth and nothing came out.

We ride the little tram from EPCOT to the parking lot, where the four of us load into the Blazer. My father puts the key in the ignition and it turns over, that familiar grinding and whirring, that familiar click of the gears as he puts it in drive. I'm crying in the backseat in the dark, holding my Figment, my impossible creature.

# CHAPTER 8

# A Knife under the Bed Will Cut the Pain

I ask my mother about my birth story. Where was she when she went into labor, when her water broke? Did my father rush her to the hospital, so frazzled that he remembered mother's suitcase but left her at the curb, the way it often happens in sitcoms? But there is not much of a story to tell. My mother was asleep during my birth, even though I came out naturally, not through a C-section. Of course she wasn't really asleep. She was just given drugs to make her not remember a thing. My mother doesn't remember pushing or anything. Her obstetrician was Dr. Elinsweig, a name that sounds like "Ellen's Wig" when you say it without the correct German pronunciation. People in Connellsville usually ignore pronunciation rules in general. Kielbasa is *ka-bossi* and a pillow is a *pilla*.

My father wasn't in the delivery room, as Dr. Elinsweig didn't like husbands observing. So I picture my dad in a fluorescent-lit waiting room, drinking vending-machine coffee from one of those dispensers where the paper cup appears out of nowhere and then a stream of coffee rains down and cream and sugar are added to your liking by mechanical arms.

My mother says her pregnancy with me was a joy from start to finish. "No morning sickness," she says. "None. And I was sick as a dog with Pam and Linda. But with you," she says, smoothing my hair with a light touch that gives me shivers, "I felt better than I'd ever felt in my life, even though I was thirty-five, which is really too old to have a baby." She was glowing for nine months straight. Strangers stopped her on the street to compliment her on her beauty. She was a knockout. "It was a sign that you would be my last child, but also my best child," she tells me. "Even in the womb, you were perfect."

I try to picture the scene of my birth—my mother perched on a hospital bed, dressed in a crinkly blue gown. She was so joyous during her final days of pregnancy with me that she painted her fingernails and toenails with bright red Revlon extra-crystalline nail polish, so her feet and hands would look pretty when she checked herself into the hospital.

"What do you mean, you checked yourself in to the hospital? Didn't you go into labor first?" I ask.

"Oh heavens, no. This was my third time around, and since it was a week past my due date, the doctor just told me to come to the hospital on November 20 and he'd take care of the rest. That was a Saturday, but I knew you would wait until after midnight." And I did. I was born at 1:31 a.m. on November 21, a Sunday. "You know what they say about the child born on the Sabbath day." My mother is talking about the fortune-telling verse that predicts the personality of a child based upon the day the child was born. The final line was her version:

> Monday's child is fair of face,
> Tuesday's child is full of grace,
> Wednesday's child is full of woe,
> Thursday's child has far to go,
> Friday's child is loving and giving,

Saturday's child works hard for a living,
But the child who is born on the Sabbath Day
Is perfectly perfect in every way.

Pam was born on a Thursday, and my mother believes this verse
is true for her, because Pam is a divorced mom who works as a waitress, who will always work as a waitress, because she chose marrying
her drunk high school sweetheart over going to college. Linda was
born on a Tuesday, and, for her, my mother thinks the verse becomes
irony. "Linda is the opposite of graceful! She's chubby and clumsy
like Zelda!" She never refers to my father's mother as *grandmother.*
Always just *Zelda.* The verse has gotten everything right when it
comes to me. I'm the blessed child, born on the blessed day.

The only detail about my birth my mother can recall with cer-
tainty is talking to a nurse about her nail polish. "I was so drugged up
and groggy. All I remember is shoving my hand at the nurse to show
her my nails, saying *It's extra extra crystalline! Extra extra crystalline!"*
My mother extends an arm to me to demonstrate, as if I'm the nurse
now. She flaps her hand in my face repeatedly, like she's showing
off a large diamond ring. "And next thing I knew, I woke up in a
recovery room and I reached down to feel my stomach and it was
already flat as a board. After Linda I was still so fat. But after you…"
She stops talking and lowers her head just a bit. She smiles without
showing any teeth. Dramatic pause. "I was just . . . " Dramatic pause.
"Beautiful."

★ ★ ★

Other than *Annie, The Wizard of Oz* is my favorite movie. It comes
on TV only one night a year. As soon as I spot the listing during my
weekly review of our home-delivered issue of *TV Guide,* I start a
countdown in my head. My favorite part of the movie is when Dorothy oils the Tin Man to set him free. He is the scariest character in

the movie, but I love him. I love his funnel-shaped head, his furnace-like body, his heavy layer of silver face paint. And even though he doesn't have a heart, he isn't cold and mean. He doesn't want to frighten people—he can't help it. When they finally get to Emerald City, the Tin Man realizes that he's had a heart all along. He just needed to learn how to use it.

My mother loves the movie, too, but her reasons are different from mine. She loves famous people who died before their time—Karen Carpenter, Marilyn Monroe, Frances Farmer, Elvis, and Judy Garland, our very own Dorothy Gale. She likes people who have died from mental problems or drug use. I think it's because they remind her of her brother Boots, the one who drank too much nerve medicine and gave himself a heart attack. My mother rations terrible stories to me like sugar in wartime. She doesn't want to use them all up at once. So she sprinkles some here and there, especially when she thinks I might want to stray from "our team." According to Mother, there are two teams in our family.

"You're just like me, Karen," she says. "We're built exactly the same."

I picture us being assembled, robots from the same factory, glass from the same mold. "What do you mean?" I ask.

"Well, every child takes after a parent. Linda takes after Dad and you take after me."

"But, I look a lot like Dad," I say. I've noticed the strong resemblance in photo after photo. We have the same jet-black hair and matching bushy eyebrows, the same fair skin and slightly elf-life ears. Linda looks more like a blend of my mother and father, her naturally curly hair much lighter than mine, the slope of her nose a bit softer.

"No, I don't mean physically. I mean mentally. You and I are the same. So it will always be me and you against Dad and Linda."

I don't see us pairing up that way, don't see the lines drawn in black and white. My father loves making up stories and even talks to my imaginary friend, whose name is Every Breevy. Mother thinks Every is a pain. She dropped a stack of clean clothes on my bed the other day and I had to tell her that she was suffocating Every. My mother just sneered. "Then tell Every to move," she said.

I imagine taking my mother to Emerald City, that cluster of green glass shining like Rolling Rock bottles in the distance. Maybe we'll get to the wizard and pull back the curtain and he'll tell me what I want to hear. *Your mother has a heart. She just needs to learn how to use it.*

# CHAPTER 9

# Red Sky in Morning, Sailors Take Warning

I am in school when it happens, so I don't see the Y-shaped cloud in real time, the way the people in the bleachers look confused, Christa McAuliffe's parents holding each other, scared. I see the scene repeated on the news that night and on *20/20*, my favorite show. I can trust Barbara Walters and Hugh Downs. I can trust the theme music, its authority, the way the date is displayed on the screen during the opening credits, proof that we are all on the same calendar. *We've grown used to wonders in this century. It's hard to dazzle us,* Ronald Reagan says in his near whisper. He's talking to me, to the children of America, telling us that the *Challenger* crew was pulling us into the future, but I don't know how they can do that now that they are dead.

At the lunch table in school, Jimmy Carter tells dirty jokes, mean jokes about Ethiopians and Peter Pan and Christa McAuliffe. "Why does Peter Pan fly?" he wants to know. He barely takes a beat, doesn't wait for a response. "If someone hit you in the peter with a pan, you'd fly, too!"

He turns to me. "What color were Christa McAuliffe's eyes?" he asks, and I know the answer, picture her image on the news, her smile through the glow of the television screen.

Whose idea was it to put a teacher in space, anyway? Seventy-three seconds, that was it. I can hardly stand to be around my mother right now because it's all she wants to talk about, the poor teacher astronaut who exploded ten miles off the ground.

I know that there are ways to control the world. I've been working on them for a while now. If I stomp my feet five times before the garage door closes, then nothing bad will happen to me. If I microwave a hot dog for eleven seconds at a time, hitting START over and over again until it is finally warm, then no more space shuttles will explode.

I don't tell my mother about the things I do to keep the world safe, but I think she understands somehow. I think she has her own ways. I think she hears the same desperate voice I hear when I'm brushing my teeth. It tells me I have to run my toothbrush across the stream of water six times, back and forth, or else. When I'm taking a drink from the water fountain at school, it tells me I must take eleven sips of water before I can stop drinking. *Do this or else. Do that or else.* It never finishes those sentences, never tells me what *or else* means.

"What color were Christa McAuliffe's eyes?" Jimmy Carter asks me again. He is agitated now. I give up the answer.

"Her eyes were blue," I say. "One blew this way, one blew that way."

★ ★ ★

It's not always the darkness itself that scares me. Sometimes it's what I see when I look inside it. In my bed at night, I stare into the black space through my open doorway. I see a man's face, always the same features—round cheeks, ruddy complexion. He wears a green knit toboggan hat. I try to see through the face, beyond it somehow, even close my eyes, but he's still there. I know he's not real, that he's not really there outside my bedroom, that he's not actually whispering my name, but it feels real, and I'm afraid to go to sleep, worried about murderers climbing through my low window. If a killer walked down the hall, my bedroom would be the first one he'd reach. I would be dead before Linda even heard a sound. She's a heavy sleeper, stretched out in her double bed, her face pressed into pillows, her baby blanket around her ears.

My bedroom is small and warm, four pink walls and one ceiling, wooden baseboards, a closet full of clothes, curtains ordered from the Sears catalog. I think I might die in this room someday, like the Clutter daughters from *In Cold Blood*. I shouldn't have read it, don't even know why old Miss Speshock, the librarian at the Carnegie Library downtown, let me check it out. I close my eyes and see the Clutter girls lying in pools of their own blood, their father dead in the furnace room atop a cardboard mattress box.

The library is a large building that looks like a cathedral of sorts—rich mahogany doorjambs and stained-glass accents on the windows. To reach some of the higher shelves of books, they have odd little wooden chairs with cranks that go round and round. You sit in the chair and crank yourself up a rusty old track to the third shelf, your feet suspended as you browse for whatever it is you're looking for. All the librarians are older than dirt and know full well that kids like to crank themselves up in the chairs for fun, so you better have a damn good reason to be doing so.

I usually go to the card catalog, feign interest in the "C" drawer, then make like I'm scribbling a call number on a small scrap of card stock they keep in a box on top. That way, in case I'm questioned, I have an alibi. But the librarians like me, as I've already established myself as a serious library patron, so they barely bat an eye when I need to hoist myself up to the third shelf. I'm usually headed to the fiction section, which is in the basement anyway, and down there the books are in two rows of shelves and you can reach them with a footstool if you need a little more height.

When I'm ready to check out, I slide a book across the smooth wooden circulation desk to Miss Speshock. She squints into her tiny eyeglasses, half moons that hang at her chest on a silver chain when not in use. Her fingers are pruny, like mine after a long bath when my mother yells at me through the door to *get out or else*. Miss Speshock fiddles with her mechanical date stamp, making sure it's set to three weeks from now. She stamps my card neatly, takes time to gently fan the ink dry before sliding the card into a brown pocket at the back of the book. Like me, Miss Speshock, knows the devil is in the details. And she's quiet. She never speaks to me, just smiles without showing any teeth, the soft lines around her mouth disappearing for just a moment.

I keep the names of various killers close to me: Sonny Hammett, Ted Bundy, James O. Huberty, Lee Harvey Oswald, Richard "Dick" Hickock. Hickock was one of the Clutter family murderers. At the end of *In Cold Blood*, he and Perry Smith are executed by hanging. It's hard to believe that they ever put people to death this way. I read Capote's description of their deaths over and over, can't get that passage out of my mind for weeks. The flailing of the legs, the thickness of the rope, how it must have dug into their skin so terribly, thick red rings around the necks of their dead bodies. How long does it take to die that way? I want to know, and I don't want to know.

When my mother talks about killing herself, it's in a less violent way. She'd walk into the river and lie down. She makes it sound peaceful, but I wonder how it would work, what would keep her from floating to the surface, her body becoming a raft pulled along the current. Where might she end up? My mother talks to me about dying another way. "If I live to be sixty-five," she tells me, "you have permission to shoot me dead. Just make it quick, okay? Right between the eyes. I'd rather be dead than old and ugly." She tells me to trust her, but I think maybe we should put it in writing, make it official, like a contract.

My mother worries about bad things happening, about kidnappings and fires and bank robberies in the middle of the day. Her worries are nothing new to me, but on this particular night she is extra agitated, her eyes unable to focus, darting all around the room as she talks to me. "Put your shoes on. We're going to see Mrs. Nesmith," she says, pulling me from the floor where I'm playing school, pretending to be teacher to an invisible class, filling page after page with the names of my students. I give them impossible names, first, middle, and last names—Sukeisha Renee Crawfish, Kitty Katherine Burkowitz, Teal Ann McGoverness.

Mrs. Nesmith is in her sixties, with two grown sons who live in Alaska and work on the pipeline. She and her husband live in a white two-story clapboard house on the corner. They have slate sidewalks, dark gray slabs you can draw on with chalk if you happen to have some in your pocket.

I ring the doorbell and Mrs. Nesmith appears, behind her a light blue glow from the television in her living room, and her husband in his recliner watching the seven o'clock news. She doesn't seem to be expecting us, but welcomes us in immediately, her face a bit alarmed. She's not used to neighbors calling in the evening like this. I am offered some gingersnaps and milk, whisked into the yellow kitchen where I sit and eat and look out the window. The sun is setting on their small backyard. They have a swing set for their Alaskan grandchildren, who visit in the summers and go swimming in our pool. Mrs. Nesmith slathers them frequently with sunblock while Linda and I bake our already golden skin in the sun.

My mother and Mrs. Nesmith (first name Heloise, like the woman who writes the famous column about household tips, such as how to take grape juice stains out of clothing) go upstairs. I don't know what they're talking about, but I hear the uneven murmur of my mother's voice mixed with the staccato of the anchorman on KDKA. Mr. Nesmith (who looks like Mr. Howell, the millionaire from *Gilligan's Island*) is snoring on and off, waking every few minutes with a snort in his recliner while the meteorologist begins talking about the weather. He uses symbols to represent cold fronts and low-pressure systems. Why did I tell that pageant host I wanted to be a secretary? I hate typing—I'm always making mistakes, my paper always clogged with Wite-Out.

I don't know how much time passes. The tiny clock on the stove doesn't work, its hands frozen at 1:35. Eventually, my mother comes downstairs to retrieve me and we walk outside. My mother and I walk side by side, my arms swinging at my sides, her arms crossed, hands nearly resting on her shoulders. It's the pose a vampire sleeps in, when he's in his coffin during daylight hours. His arms are crossed to protect him from stakes through the heart, in case someone wishes to kill him in his sleep. We're so vulnerable when we sleep, just as my mother and I are vulnerable walking back to our house in near darkness. The streetlights haven't turned themselves on yet. I imagine a man approaching us from behind, one gloved hand over my mouth. My pace quickens.

"I feel better now," Mother says as we walk around the back of the house, enter the kitchen through the sliding-glass door. "Mrs. Nesmith says it's okay to worry the way I do." She starts wiping down the already clean kitchen counters while she talks. It's pure mechanical movement, as though she is a windup doll and someone has just turned the key on her back. "Mrs. Nesmith said I don't worry about *the impossible*. I worry about *the highly improbable*. And that's entirely healthy, because there's a difference between the two and why not be prepared for the highly improbable?" She's down on her hands and knees now, scrubbing the linoleum with an S.O.S pad, leaving streaks of blue foam in her wake.

I run through the fears and worries I've been cataloging in my head for as long as I can remember. My memory begins and ends with fear. Men breaking into our house at night and killing us—highly improbable. But certainly not impossible. My father having a heart attack—highly improbable. Aliens abducting me—highly improbable. An ax murderer lurking under my bed at night, just waiting for me to dangle one foot off the side—highly improbable. But nothing is impossible.

I grab the bucket and a washrag from under the kitchen sink, fill the bucket halfway with clean water. I get down on the wet floor next to my mother and follow her. I rinse her work away until the whole floor is spotless and shining.

# PART TWO

*I remember wanting—red licorice shining through a glass case, the neon red arrow above the drive-in entrance. We have the scratchy speaker attached to our car, our windows rolled down in summer. The movie starts at dusk. Until then, I play on the swing set, holding rusty chains that seem to crumble in my grasp, flecks of red and brown embedded in my palms. I want things. A canopy bed, a Siamese cat, ballet shoes with pink ribbons I can tie around my ankles, the red licorice. I beg my father to buy it for me, and eat the whole package, my lips stained red and raw by the end of a film I don't recall seeing. Images move across a giant screen, the light projected from a little shack. For a moment, I see the outline of a man inside. He sits behind the square window, loading spools of invisible film. I remember his silhouette, the slant of his hat, the thatched roof.*

*The next morning, I'm in yellow underwear and nothing else, throwing up in the bathroom sink while my mother gets ready for work. A red stream splashes inside the powder blue basin, circles the drain. Our toothbrushes stare silently in a row, anchored to a ceramic holder on the blue tile of the bathroom wall. It's hard to think of anything else, so I remember wanting. I remember desire.*

# CHAPTER 10

# Break a Mirror, Bury the Pieces

I'm sitting on the back porch, my bare legs brushing the green out-door carpet, the kind that covers Green Garden Miniature Golf on Route 119, and looks like it's made of plastic. Green Garden has a windmill and a wooden airplane with propellers. You must hit a col-ored ball between the blades. They have sand traps, and water haz-ards, and a final hole where your ball disappears into a noisy white pipe, making a clanging sound as it travels down under the ground. I wonder if it can get lost, end up in the sewer somehow. How does it know where to go? How does anything know where it belongs?

I've made my mother angry today, so I've been sent out here on the porch to sit in the sun, to think about what I've done. My mother has beautiful things on her dresser, things I'm not supposed to touch. Some she uses and others are for decoration only, her fake plants, her greenery. My mother dusts her greenery with lemon Pledge. She sprays it directly on the leaves, then wipes them with a soft rag, which is actually a piece of old T-shirt. Every few months, mother cuts up one of my father's work T-shirts into rags. They are thin from too many washes, and I want to steal one for myself, hide it in my drawer and touch it to my face every so often, when I can't fall asleep at night, when the house creaks and I wonder if it's a man breaking into our home, when I look into the dark hall outside my bedroom doorway and see the face staring back at me. When I have to knock on wood every time I think in my head *nothing bad happens to me, nothing bad happens to me,* those times when I need something to hold on to.

I love everything on top of my mother's dresser—the brush, comb, and mirror set with heavy bronze handles, the vanity tray with scalloped gold edges, the box of scented powder from Estée Lauder that comes with a square powder puff, fluffy white, a length of ribbon on the outside. You slide your hand between the ribbon and the puff, as if you're sliding your hand into a luxurious mitten. Then you pat it all over your body, making small chalky clouds around you, the scent of flowers and spice in the air. There are glass bottles of nail polish, various shades of pink, glass bottles of perfume, expensive face creams in jars with heavy lids, trinkets and knick-knacks. There's a tiny pewter jewelry box that holds my grandparents' class rings, years etched on the side, letters that stand for something, although I'm not sure what, and some sort of Navy pin that belonged to my Uncle Little Joe.

I'm not supposed to touch anything on my mother's dresser, but I like to pretend as though I'm in a commercial, and her dresser is the only spot in the house that will do as my sound stage. There's a large mirror, and I stare into it. It is my camera. I can sit at the edge of my parents' bed and tell my audience how youthful and soft my hands look and feel because I use Nivea. I can share stories of men who follow me around, thanks to the scent of my Youth Dew perfume, how strong my nails are thanks to Sally Hansen. I've done commercials plenty of times and no one's ever noticed. I usually wait until everyone has made themselves scarce—maybe someone's at work or at the store, maybe someone's downstairs watching television, maybe Linda is at Rochelle's house. But today my mother finds me somehow. I don't remember how now, the details already fuzzy, but she has found me and she is angry now, and the mirrored tray with scalloped gold edges is broken, the bottles of nail polish are broken—some spilled on the mint-green carpet in my parents' bedroom, some on my legs. I watch it shimmer on my skin, here in the sun, on the back porch, where I am supposed to be thinking about what I have done.

My father comes home from fishing and finds me here and for a moment, I act as if nothing is wrong. "I'm just getting some air," I say. But then he goes inside and my mother must tell him something. I can't hear what they are saying through the closed  windows, but a few minutes later my father comes out to get me.

"We're going for a drive," he says.

"Where?" I ask. And "What about Linda?"

"We'll pick her up on our way."

I go inside through the patio door and see my mother sitting at the dining room table, staring straight ahead, her eyes like marbles, the cloudy ones they call cat's eyes. She is twisting a dishrag in her hands, her arms close to her body, stiff, a doll's immovable parts. My father touches her shoulder, a signal for her to stand, which she does mechanically, not looking at me. We walk outside and into the Lincoln, the dishrag still in her hands, always in her hands, as my father drives to Rochelle's to pick up Linda, who gets in the car bewildered, until I signal to her with my eyes, let her know that Mother is having a spell, a phrase we've heard our father use somewhere before, though we're not sure where.

We drive to Ohiopyle, up the mountain, to where the Youghiogheny makes a small double waterfall, where people kayak and ride bicycles and eat ice cream in the summer, look at golden leaves in the fall, watch the frozen river in the winter.

"Do you want to park and get out? To see the falls?" my father asks my mother. She doesn't answer, but twirls the dishrag, which must mean *no*. So my father keeps driving, down windy roads that make me feel carsick, but I don't dare say a word about it. Usually, I sit in the front seat on long trips, because the Lincoln rides like a magic carpet, as if its wheels don't even touch the ground, and I get queasy if I'm not able to get a clear view out the front windshield. I try to look through the crack between my mother's head and the car door, a small sliver of clear glass. I find a decent position and sit that way the rest of the ride home, perfectly still, not even breathing too heavy, not wishing to disturb my mother, not wishing to make the spell worse, not wishing for anything anymore.

★ ★ ★

I'm in fifth grade now, in Mrs. McLuckey's class. I guess you could say I'm the teacher's pet. Mrs. McLuckey says she and I are on the same wavelength. I picture us in a little boat together, rowing over our thoughts that are clear and cool like water. When Mrs. McLuckey has papers to grade, she asks me to read aloud to the class from whatever book we're currently reading—*A Wrinkle in Time, Bridge to Terabithia, Island of the Blue Dolphins*. I like Judy Blume books but not *Are You There God, It's Me, Margaret,* like every other girl in class. My favorites are *Deenie* and *Tiger Eyes*. Amy and I are still best friends, and she's turning me on to Stephen King. Her mom has a whole collection of fat paperbacks, the spines worn out from folding. I'm starting with *Carrie*. Amy says that is a good place to start.

There's a new girl in school this year. She transferred from the Catholic elementary school in town. She is tall like me, but thinner and freckled. She has long red hair that is very bright, the color of carrots. Her name is Heather Grain. There are lots of girls named Heather and Jennifer and Amanda in my grade, but Heather Grain seems different. Everyone wants to be her friend, even though they know little about her. In the movies and on TV the new kid has a hard time fitting in, but not Heather Grain. It's like she was born to be here, right here in this classroom, born to be popular. I've been trying to figure out popularity since kindergarten, when it was already clear that Amy and I would never be popular, and kids like Amanda Weaver and Todd Armor would break records for the most-loved children in town.

Heather Grain is always staring at me. I catch her every now and then. I turn my head and she suddenly snaps her eyes back to the front of the room, pretends like she's copying something from the chalkboard, but Mrs. McLuckey hasn't even written anything down. All the girls are chattering more this year, about bras and makeup and growing-up things. I'd noticed the change in Linda that began when she hit fifth grade. When Rochelle would come over they'd talk about boys and kissing. They'd read magazines and point to pictures, giggling at each other to communicate instead of using words.

Then one night, toward the end of Linda's fifth-grade year, my mother called her over to the couch, and together they read through a pink booklet about becoming a woman. It had a cartoon drawing of a girl on the front and the words were actually written in ribbon. I looked for the booklet in Linda's room a few days later. I like to snoop through her drawers when she goes to Rochelle's house. I never found it.

The girls are giggling this week because we're going to watch the puberty video, which everyone is just calling the period video because we can't imagine what else there is to talk about. Jimmy Carter promises to tell us girls all the explicit details of the boys' puberty video, which he says will be about boners and wet dreams and jacking off.

The period film they show us stars Andrea McArdle, the original Annie on Broadway. She explains, at times through song, that all of our body parts have a necessary function. We need lungs for breathing, a heart to circulate blood, and a uterus to bear children.

We watch a cartoon graphic of the uterine lining thickening up each month, preparing for the egg, followed by tiny contractions that flush the unused tissue outside the body when the egg isn't fertilized.

Andrea tells us other things—that it's okay to bathe or shower during our periods and that we need to start washing our hair more often and wearing deodorant. It turns out that our skin is about to start making more oil, which we all think is pretty disgusting. I find it strange that a girl who played Annie is telling me about the difference between maxi pads and panty liners. We get little pink bags with samples of both as we leave the library, shove them into our desks quickly once we're back in the classroom.

At lunch, Jimmy Carter lives up to his promise. "Our film had Mickey Mouse in it," he says, then imitates the cartoon character's high-pitched voice. "Hey boys, you're going to grow hair on your balls!" I know he's not telling the truth, but the other boys have been sworn to secrecy. They're backing Jimmy up as usual.

My mother circles certain days with a red pen in her pocket calendar, the one she gets every year from the card store. The plastic cover is usually decorated in flowers or the "Footprints in the Sand" picture and verse she loves. She can read that verse over and over again and it still gets her every time. I don't understand the appeal. So God was carrying the guy through the hard times, that's why there was only one set of footprints. Big deal. It's not so hard to figure that one out the first time around.

Where are the other girls like me? Amy might be one of them, but she doesn't seem to have the same strange insides as I do, the odd thoughts and worries. My mother says worrying is a family trait. Her mother was a worrier. That's how she ended up in a mental hospital in Worthington, Ohio, receiving electroshock therapy. She had what they called nervous breakdowns back then. I know that I'm nervous, too, but I don't think I've ever had a breakdown, although I have had some days where I feel like I'm slipping down a drain. When I finally reach the bottom, it takes some time for me to climb back out. I tell my mother about these feelings and there's a light of recognition in her eyes. Maybe we are alike after all.

My mother wants to know about my slipping down the drain— what it feels like, what triggers it. She wants us to sit on her bed and have long conversations about these things, just us, our secret talks. My mother says she feels doomed sometimes. I nod my head in agreement. "It's not so much that I want to die, but it feels like I'm doomed to die," she says. "It feels like maybe it would be easier if I were to lie down in the river. Just to get it over with. Do you understand?" I am eleven years old. I understand.

Sometimes, my mother feels like crying for no reason at all. I find her one afternoon, spread across her polyester bedspread, one arm over her forehead. She's got tears in her eyes, and I want to know what's wrong. "Nothing's wrong," she says. "You don't have to have a reason to cry. You can cry just because you want to."

I want to show my mother that I'm just like her. She needs that. And it's the least I can do. I stare at the bronze butterflies on the wall, the small plaque of the Ten Commandments. *Honor thy father and mother*, it says. I think about something sad, like my father dying. I think about what this house would be like without him, and I cry. I don't cry for him—I cry for me, the child left behind with her mother.

# CHAPTER 11

# Never Bring an Old Broom into a New House

The summer after fifth grade, we're eating fruit salad on the back porch—three girls spread out on different pieces of green and yellow vinyl furniture. Linda and Rochelle have already picked out all the strawberries, oranges, and grapes, leaving me with the bananas and apples, which are turning brown from air exposure. Our mother makes fruit salad only once every summer, though we beg for it regularly as soon as the temperature hits eighty degrees. *It's too damn expensive, and you guys never save any for me* is her standard reply. Part of this statement is true.

My mother loves summer. She loves tanning in the tri-fold lounge chair by the pool, the kind that leaves deep grooves on the backs of her thighs when she gets up. She loves spritzing herself with water from the plant sprayer, drinking industrial-strength lemonade out of a giant Tupperware tumbler. *The recipe is easy,* she assures me. *Two lemons, two cups of sugar, ice, and water to fill.*

Because of her work schedule, my mother misses most of the best tanning days, like today, when the radio DJ reminds you to turn yourself over every thirty minutes with a kitchen timer sound effect, a high-pitched ding that makes me think of the show I'm addicted to right now in black-and-white reruns: *The Donna Reed Show*. Donna is often in the kitchen, a sheer half apron over her full-skirted dress, the delicate ding from the spotless electric range reminding her to take out the meatloaf. The timer on my mother's oven sounds more like a buzzing alarm clock.

Linda and Rochelle are talking about soon-to-be ninth-grade boys with simple names like John, Jim, and Eddie. They think they're being sly about it, but I know they're talking about a game of Spin the Bottle played in Rochelle's basement. Every house in our neighborhood has a basement, sometimes called a game room: an underground lair where kids and teenagers get themselves into trouble and generally hide from adults, who prefer to live at ground level.

"I can't believe you landed on Eddie!" Rochelle says. "Lucky duck." She pulls at her bikini top, which is white and dotted with tiny rainbows. I'm wearing a bronze one-piece Speedo my mother bought at the sporting goods store. It fits like second skin and makes me look like a shiny turd.

Linda and Rochelle are playing Gin Rummy, a game they refuse to teach me. Linda is winning. Our father is at the factory and our mother is out shopping, so we can't so much as dip a toe in the pool and are sequestered to the porch for now. We're not allowed to swim without an adult home, even if the adult home is downstairs reading *Field & Stream*, or in the bathroom bleaching her hair. *At least someone will be there to hear you scream,* my mother insists.

We've had the swimming pool since I was in first grade. My mother used the little lump of money she inherited from her dead father to have it built. For weeks, Linda and I got to watch shirtless sunburned men turn our backyard into a muddy hole. They created an intricate network of wires, bleached white gravel underneath. I helped by hauling around tin trays of salted watermelon slices and offering them Coke in frosty bottles.

The biggest commotion was the day the cement truck arrived. Kids from all over the neighborhood came by to hang over our fence and watch gray sludge slide down a red metal chute and into the hole. You could smell the wet concrete in the air, hear the soft *whoosh* of it being poured, then combed, then swept with what looked like a giant broom. My father took photos with his 35mm to catalog each step of the process. My mother says the developed roll looks like "construction pornography."

My mother always wanted an in-ground swimming pool, but only the cement kind, not the kind with blue plastic lining, which looks tacky. And it had to be kidney shaped with Roman steps, not rectangular or oval. Rich People have kidney-shaped pools with Roman steps. Rich People is a group to which my mother wants to belong, but because she and my father are lifelong factory workers, she is grooming me to be a Rich Person instead. There aren't many Rich People in Connellsville, so she and I watch *Lifestyles of the Rich and Famous* for research, which has helped me develop a dead-on impersonation of Robin Leach, even though the only thing I can say in his voice is "I'm Robin Leach!"

As they play cards, Linda and Rochelle go on and on about soon-to-be ninth-grade boys, while I quickly lose my desire to figure out who and what they're talking about. I don't care much about soon-to-be sixth-grade boys either. Right now, they don't seem to be good for much, except teasing me about my hairy arms or the fact that I named my cat Charmin. They all want to know if I wipe my ass with her. It's the beginning of summer and I don't want to think of anything school related right now.

I peel myself off the vinyl lounge chair, enjoying the sound of my skin as it un-sticks, and walk over to the wooden fence that separates our yard from our neighbor's. "Hey, you guys," I say to Linda and Rochelle. "There's a moving truck in front of Mr. Nicola's!" Linda and Rochelle aren't impressed. They're now flipping through some teen magazines, pointing to pictures and mouthing words to each other, their eyes big as dinner plates.

Mr. Nicola lived next door to us all my life, minus the last few months, during which time the house has been empty, Mr. Nicola having died in April. He was old and quiet, and I only saw him in the warmer months when he tended to his backyard garden in a wide-brimmed straw hat, or hauled a tiny trash bag to the alley in black kneesocks and shorts. He wore those little elastic bands around his calves to keep his socks up. Mr. Nicola had an old-fashioned bird-cage full of blue and yellow parakeets positioned in his front picture window.

I'd walk by the birds on my way to visit Krissy Page, who is a year younger than me and used to live at the top of our street. I didn't visit her very often because my mother thought she was too dumb to be my friend. *She's in remedial classes, for God's sake!* she'd remind me. The birds were always flapping around to their various perches and swings, their chirps vibrating through the thin glass.

After Mr. Nicola died, his son Elmer (*like the glue* he told me when we met) came back to Pennsylvania from Georgia, where he lives with a wife and two daughters, to clean out and sell the house. My mother invited him over one evening for instant coffee and a hushed conversation around the ashtray we keep in the attic crawlspace for our smoking guests. It's orange and white and shaped like a mushroom, the ash collecting in its curved ceramic belly.

For weeks Linda and I got to watch all sorts of oddities carried out of our neighbor's house, an old two-story with green aluminum siding and black wrought-iron railings, as Elmer had an estate sale. We weren't allowed to go over and look at the stuff, even though I spotted practically everyone from our block come out with something interesting—a set of rose-tinted drinking glasses, a black wicker footstool, a large silver-framed mirror with scalloped edges.

*It's simply uncouth,* my mother said. *Circling around the dead like god-damn vultures.* The birdcage and the birds ended up in the backseat of Elmer's orange Ford station wagon, the kind with wood grain panels on the sides, destined for Georgia.

On Elmer's final day in Connellsville, my mother rounded Linda and me up to walk next door with her and deliver a homemade zucchini bread wrapped in waxed paper. *To take home to your girls,* she told him. He smiled and thanked her, then offered my sister and me a chance to roam around the empty place while they talked. I immediately ran for the thick mahogany staircase. While our house has a basement, and, therefore, stairs leading down to it, we don't have such a grand example of a genuine staircase. Our stairs are really more of a tunnel that leads underground, a rectangular shaft you have to walk down single file. Mr. Nicola's house has the kind with a smooth banister you can slide down like kids do in movies. I walked to the top of the steps, resisting the urge to sling one leg over the railing. Rich People don't slide down banisters.

Linda and Rochelle are sick of sitting outside on the sticky porch chairs. They're going inside, giant beach towels wrapped around them, to watch *Dirty Dancing* on video for the hundredth time. We all have crushes on Johnny, Patrick Swayze's character in the movie—a tough guy from the wrong side of the tracks who has muscles and sexy dance moves and perfectly styled hair. He wears tight black tank tops that show off his toned shoulders. I have a poster of Patrick Swayze in my bedroom. He's half sitting, half lying down, leaning on one perfect elbow, staring at me.

The new neighbors begin unloading their truck full of boxes and furniture. I catch a glimpse of a few boys running inside, hoping they're around my age. They won't know I named my cat after toilet paper, that I cried on stage when I accidentally misspelled the word "practical" during the fifth-grade spelling bee, that Heather

Grain yelled out "Crybaby!" from the audience and all the kids laughed. That I fell in the cafeteria once, chili splattering the dull gray linoleum while everyone applauded. The house next door starts to breathe, as they fling open every window. I hear the low murmur of voices, imagine boys running up the heavy stairs, then sliding down.

# CHAPTER 12

# Tie a Red Ribbon on a Sick Child

I'm getting too old to play with dolls. Rows of Cabbage Patch Kids sit on plastic shelves in my bedroom, soft cloth bodies in diapers, hard faces, iris stickers for eyes, chubby feet stuffed into baby socks and hard little shoes. They don't say a word, but they watch me in my bed, when I'm doing things I shouldn't, like rubbing myself to reach the dew point. When I'm finished, I roll over to face the wall, so the dolls can't see me.

My cat sleeps on my bed with me every night, starting out at my feet, but ending up near my head at some point, the soft pads of her paws sometimes waking me as she tries to make a nest in my hair. She loves me and only me, sleeps on my bed all day while I'm in school, next to my Alvin the Chipmunk doll and blankie, the little afghan my mother made for me before I was born. Blankie is soft from washing, and I love when it's hot from the dryer, smelling like fabric softener and warm air. I'm certain different temperatures have different smells. You can smell cold, just like you can smell hot, and every degree in between.

I'm starting the sixth grade in the fall, so I'm too old to play with dolls, just like I'm too old to play with our new neighbor, who is going into the third grade, but he has become my best friend this summer, my only friend. My mother finally scared away Amy Nickels when she checked Amy's head for lice before letting her come inside to play with me one afternoon. My mother has decided that our new neighbor doesn't have lice. He likes to play dolls with me, and he doesn't mind if I paint his nails or put mousse in his hair.

His name is Samuel Ryan. He has two older brothers in high school, named Greg and Danny, and one younger sister, Sarah, who goes to a special school in Uniontown. Sarah needs more help than the special education kids at our elementary school, the kids who learn in a basement classroom, who only come up for air at lunchtime, where the other kids laugh at them under their breath, and call them "speds" behind their backs. One boy's head is permanently cocked to one side, like the dog in the RCA ads, peering into the horn of the phonograph, his head tilted, black ears listening intently. I don't know this kid's real name, but I call him "Amos" in my mind. Another kid can't seem to close his mouth. It's constantly open and he wears a terry-cloth bib to absorb his drool.

Sarah is seven years old. Her head is very small, almond shaped, her eyes round and black, only her pupils visible. She still wears diapers, and sometimes, when she hops the fence to play with us, she smells terrible and Samuel has to remind her to go home and ask their mom to change her. Sarah will get angry for a moment, but will eventually climb the fence again, emerge minutes later shouting "I came over!"

My mother has little patience for retarded people, so I'm proud of her for behaving herself about Sarah and Samuel, holding my breath sometimes when it seems she might say something mean. She wants to blame Samuel's parents for Sarah. Surely they must have done something to make her that way. After a few weeks of the Ryan family living next door, my mother finally comes up with a hypothesis.

When two people get together and have a really intelligent child (Danny, who is Linda's age and the smartest kid in their class), it only makes sense that they are also capable of making a really stupid child.

Mrs. Ryan, whose first name is Alicia, even though it doesn't fit her face in the slightest, is always in a bad mood. She looks more like a Helen or a Martha to me. She's a manager at a fast-food restaurant and works the overnight shift, her red Chevy Lumina pulling into the makeshift parking spot in their backyard in the morning. She opens the car door slowly, toting a Styrofoam cup of coffee, waving half heartedly to me and Samuel, as we can often be found sitting on the glider on my back porch in the light of the rising sun, waiting for the summer air to warm so we can go swimming.

Greg is the oldest and a senior in high school. His bedroom window is the only window in their house that faces ours, and most nights in the summer, Greg takes the screen out and sits on his windowsill, listening to a Richard Marx tape, one leg dangling outside. He usually rewinds "Don't Mean Nothing" a few times, listens to it again for good measure. Danny is the middle brother and a genius. According to a rumor, he has the highest IQ of all the kids in IMPACT in the school district, so he thinks he's smarter than me.

Greg and Danny and Samuel and Sarah come over some afternoons to watch HBO in the basement with Linda and me. It's very hot this summer, but our basement is always cool. It's below ground, with one window that looks out into my mother's flower bed, which is more like a gravel bed these days, as she's given up on growing anything. She loves her plastic greenery more, would rather polish it than try to nurture a living thing. After a while, the six of us get bored and go outside and throw ourselves on the white hot driveway, where Samuel and I get out a box of chalk and begin to draw stick-figure versions of ourselves. Greg draws a naked woman, complete with nipples and pubic hair. Linda makes an elephant, the only thing she knows how to draw.

Danny writes Einstein's equation for the theory of relativity, $E=mc^2$. I let him have his moment, pretending not to know that E stands for energy, m for mass, c for the speed of light in a vacuum, pretending not to know that energy and mass are transmutable, that it's always possible to change one form, nature, substance, or state into another. Pretending not to know that ideas are translatable into reality, like atoms sharing electrons, covalent bonds, like kids on concrete sharing this longing, this tension that powders the air around us, the chalk dust settling as we draw.

★ ★ ★

Samuel and I swim in our pool every day. Some nights we swim after it gets dark, dragging ourselves out of the warm water at nine, ten, even eleven o'clock, and say goodbye. Some nights I fall asleep on the couch in the basement, still in my bathing suit, my hair tangled in a ponytail that smells like chlorine. I wake up and wade into the pool before I even eat breakfast. Some mornings, Samuel is sitting on his back porch, waiting for me to come out. Some mornings, I wait for him. One of us is always there, killing time until the other emerges, as if we can't think of anything else to do, as if there is nothing to do without the other.

We invent our own world in the water, hang beach towels over the diving board, letting the ends of the towels dip into the water, becoming heavy and dense. Inside this space we create a tiny spaceship. We close the imaginary door and lift off. When we come out, we are on another planet, a planet that looks much like Earth, but is completely covered in water. My family's dog, a cocker spaniel poodle mix named Honey Louise runs around the edge of the pool when we play. We call her Shultz, the Underwater Space Dog, make her a part of our adventure.

Linda doesn't like our game, because she feels Honey Louise is her dog, and she doesn't like the fact that the dog runs to us when we call her Shultzie, the tags on her collar jingling, her claws clicking the damp pavement around the pool. Linda thinks we're brainwashing her dog and she won't stand for it. But there's nothing she can do, because I am powerful when I am with Samuel. He and I together are somehow greater than the sum of our child bodies.

Samuel knows what I like, makes a point to remember things about me. He knows my favorite Kool-Aid flavor is tropical punch. He knows I love the soundtrack to *Dirty Dancing*. He knows that I secretly wish I had a childhood disease, like leukemia or cystic fibrosis, not because I want to die, but because I want attention, want my family to gather around my bed holding my hands and placing cool washcloths on my face. Samuel knows that I have never kissed a boy, that I adore doo-wop music from the 1950s, my mother's 8-track tapes we listen to, sprawled out on the couches in the basement while we eat peanut butter and jelly sandwiches—no crusts for Samuel.

Their father, Greg Senior, works at the mill in Clairton, and he has to work a lot of overtime to afford Sarah's special school. Alicia has to work a lot, too, but I get the feeling it's more to avoid being at home than anything else. The older brothers are left in charge of Samuel and Sarah a lot. I like to go over to their house on these days. Greg and Danny and Samuel are the Lost Boys and I am Wendy Darling, Sarah our female Peter Pan. She will never grow up. Alicia told my mother that Sarah will never develop fine motor skills, never be able to write her name or tie her shoes. Sarah sits at the kitchen table, scribbling long ragged strokes on her fish sticks with a blue Crayola marker before eating them, shoving them in her mouth with a satisfying look, her cheeks puffy with breading and shards of fish meat.

I show Samuel the secrets of his house—how you can take the ball off the end of the banister, pretend it's an old-fashioned telephone. That's what the Nicola grandkids and I used to do on the days we ran around this old house, the days Mr. and Mrs. Nicola were still alive. They rarely allowed their grandkids to go swimming in our pool, afraid they would drown, even though they were all strong swimmers. They wanted them to stay home and eat toasted cheese sandwiches and watch the birds in their cage.

I show Samuel the hidden door in Greg's room, the crawl space inside the wallpapered wall that no one knows about. Inside we find an empty jewelry box shaped like a treasure chest, tarnished gold chains that stretch to keep the lid open. We promise not to tell anyone, just like we promise not to tell anyone about the day we almost lost Sarah, how we took her to the playground and didn't pay attention to her. How she must have wandered down the street. How we called for her. How she finally came running from out of nowhere. How she couldn't tell us where she'd been.

★ ★ ★

In our house, we float in separate bubbles, my mother's tinged with factory grease, my father's quiet, invisible sometimes. We can go for days without noticing one another, only passing each other in the hallway, down the basement stairs, around the dining room table, piles of food on top of plates on top of a pink vinyl tablecloth with flannel backing. My mother cleans up after mealtime, won't allow anyone else to do so. She needs a place for everything, everything in its place, the spoons stacked in a certain order inside the silverware drawer, butter knives and sharp knives separated, the jagged edges never allowed to touch the smooth. Even in the cupboards, canned goods sleep in orderly rows, all the labels facing the same way, canisters always filled to the top, flour and sugar packed like snow.

Samuel's house is our opposite. Stepping inside is like entering a playground of dust and clutter. Noisy and bright, the windows are always open in summer. They are a loud family. I can hear them arguing and celebrating when I sit on our back porch with Honey Louise. Sometimes, Samuel's mother gets angry, fed up with her boys and their boy messes, fed up with changing Sarah's diapers, fed up with working the night shift at the drive-thru, the constant opening and closing of the accordion window, handing out grease-stained paper bags, cheeseburgers in their slippery yellow wrappers, Styrofoam boxes of chicken nuggets, super-sized drinks.

Once, she swiped some kids' meal toys for me and Samuel—a plastic sleeve of french fries that turned into a robot, a milk shake with secret panels. We played with our food transformers in Samuel's sandbox, first burying them, and then making them emerge like heroes to save us.

It is nearly September now, and my father is preparing to close the pool. Samuel and I watch as he pumps a foot of water from it, a chlorine stream running down the gravel alley and into a drain. Our first summer together is almost over, although I'll never say those words out loud, never give a name to what is happening around me, afraid that if I dare to speak it, it will all disappear. Afraid that Samuel isn't real at all, that he's the ghost boy I invented to love, to love me back. I want to knock on wood when I think about Samuel and me. I want to throw salt over my shoulder into the eyes of the devil I feel standing behind us, waiting.

When you spill salt, you must toss some over your shoulder. But you can't just pick up the saltshaker and shake it. You have to use the spilled salt, have to pinch it between the forefinger and thumb of your right hand, toss it over your left shoulder. This is the way my mother does it. This is the only way it works.

My mother is a book of superstitions, an encyclopedia I open daily, running my index finger down the pages looking for definitions, for instructions. If you swallow twelve cat hairs, you will die. If a bird flies into your house, someone you know will die within twenty-four hours. If you eat twelve grapes at midnight on New Year's Eve, one for each strike of the clock, you will have good fortune in the coming year. If you see a shooting star, someone you love will die. I look things up in her, my dictionary of what-if's, of how-to's, my mother, my own atlas, map of the world.

★ ★ ★

School starts. Leaves and fallen buckeyes collect at our feet as we walk. I am in sixth grade now, Samuel in third. I'm worried that people will think we're boyfriend and girlfriend. The idea embarrasses me, even though it is something I want more than anything else. If only we were older, then age wouldn't matter so much. If I were twenty-three and Samuel were twenty, we could get married and no one would think we were weird. Samuel doesn't seem to care that I have dark hair on my legs and arms, and he doesn't know that my classmates have teased me about it over the years, told me I was turning into a gorilla, that I was turning into a man. He doesn't know that my mother wouldn't buy me deodorant in fifth grade, even though I needed it, and that I had to go to school smelling like body odor, because the baby powder I patted on my armpits wore off after a few hours.

Samuel doesn't know that Heather Grain would whisper about me, about how bad I smelled, how the girls in class would secretly warn each other not to sit next to me. He doesn't know that last year, a boy named Brad Molan followed me home from school, harassed me the entire way about my hairy arms, laughing and snorting and pushing on his glasses as they slid down his sweaty nose, how I found out later that Heather Grain put him up to it, how I still don't understand why she hates me so much, why she gives me death stares in the lunchroom, tells other kids not to be my friend.

I'm happy at school once a week, when I'm placed in a van and shuttled to IMPACT, where I learn about special things and people like Brad and Heather aren't allowed to come. My mother tells me that I'm destined for greatness, that some day I'll get my revenge as I sit on the couch next to Johnny Carson on *The Tonight Show* and then I can finally reveal the names of my childhood tormentors, make them feel bad for teasing me. Then my phone will ring off the hook with people apologizing. "They'll be kissing your ass," my mother says. "Just wait and see."

I don't know what will make me famous enough to sit on the couch at *The Tonight Show*, so I'll wait and I'll see. My fame is the answer in one of Carnac the Magnificent's envelopes. One day I'll be torn open, and the rest of my story will be revealed, a prediction come true.

Samuel and I like to take pictures of each other. We pose in front of the landscaped shrubbery around the swimming pool, try to capture action shots of us jumping off the brick wall that runs next to the driveway. We take pictures of Honey Louise running, her ears pinned back in the wind. We pose on the diving board, even though the pool is closed now for the winter, sleeping under a dark green tarp my father has anchored with long water bags. The bags remind me of the rubber hot water bottle my mother pulls from the bathroom closet when someone gets the flu. It swells like a hot pregnant belly when you fill it and you have to cover it with a towel so it won't burn your skin.

Sometimes, the red caps on the poolside water bags flip open, clear water shooting straight up like small fountains, reminding me of what Old Faithful might look like in miniature. I love anything built to scale: model cars, model houses, doll furniture, blueprints of cities, where every tree, every flower is planned to the centimeter.

I lead a double life. In school, I am a Goody Two-Shoes. Quiet, teacher's pet, nothing less than an A in every subject, no friends, no one to trade clothing and glances with. No one to get in trouble with. At home, I am Samuel's wife, a child bride longing to grow up, Samuel and I playing house, Sarah our staccato child. We care for her together, defend her when a group of mean kids outside the corner store calls her a retard.

Is Samuel too young to realize what I want? Or has he figured out that I'm wishing to be kissed, pretending that we're lovers when we hide under his back porch steps, pretending that he's going to kiss me at any moment, pretending that he wants to kiss me? In the basement, I listen to my mother's records, Crystal Gayle and Anne Murray and Air Supply, anything sad, anything about love.

★ ★ ★

I think I would die for my mother. She loves dead people. They are quiet, invisible. Dead people don't live inside tombs and under gravestones, they live in the mind, in the body. Her brothers, her mother, her father, they are liquid, moving—she can conjure them anytime. She can talk to them and she can make them talk back to her. This is why she loves them.

She loves Elvis so much, and he is dead, too. I like to study her Elvis bottles in the basement, whiskey decanters she collects, in different Elvis shapes and Elvis sizes. They hold whiskey but also play music, something to listen to while you drink. I pick one up, turn it over, twist the small silver key underneath. High-pitched bells plink out a melody *hup two, three, four, occupation G.I. blues.* Elvis is in his army fatigues, tall black boots, leaning against a duffle bag full of letters, "Presley" in block print on a patch over his heart. His hair is slicked back, but dry in porcelain. When the music stops, I turn him over again, listening first to the whiskey splashing inside his hollow body, then to the bells replaying their tune. The song starts out fast, but gets slower as the key unwinds, as the musical parts lose their momentum, that system of raised metal dots spinning, a turbine powered by Braille.

I think of my mother crying when Elvis died, mascara down her face, her throat dry from sobbing as she listened to *Are You Lonesome Tonight?* on the turntable. It was August 1977, and our house didn't have air-conditioning yet so surely all of the windows were open. My father returned home from work, found my mother sobbing on the living room floor. Surely I was hot and sticky in my crib, shaking the bars to get out. Surely the song floated out of our house, passed like air through the freshly washed screens, into a world where Elvis was dead, where my mother had lost someone she adored.

I have a musical jewelry box in my bedroom. It's in the shape of a Swiss chalet painted blue and white. Tiny pink flowers live in the window boxes. I imagine it is a sweet shop, where they sell saltwater taffy and chocolate bunnies year-round (not just at Easter). I can't figure out why a ballerina appears when I open the roof. What is she doing there, trapped in perpetual spin, her spindly legs glued together, inseparable?

Her tutu is a stiff piece of net and I can undress her, slide the skirt over her head and watch her dance naked, arms permanently in third position, the ballet poses I'd memorized years before in dance class, a dozen girls in black leotards and baby fat, chanting as our arms and legs move through each one, *first, second, third, fourth,* rising on tiptoe for fifth, so high on Orange Crush from the soda machine in the waiting room we thought we might take flight.

The ballerina has no face. It sounds impossible, but I'm looking at her now and she has no face, just a plastic head without features, without color. She can't leave the sweet shop. Elvis can't stop reading that sack of letters he's leaning on. I can't die for my mother. Each of us can only do what we've been designed to do. I'm afraid I've been designed to live.

# CHAPTER 13

# If You Sing before Seven

We sing sad songs in chorus. *Some say love, it is a river that drowns the tender reed.* I am an alto, singing harmony. We are the low voices that carry more sadness than the soprano girls'. I envy their feminine-sounding melodic lines and desperately want to sing their part, thinking that being an alto means that I am part-boy, that I have too many male hormones. Most days, my body feels like a puzzle. Some pieces fit, while others don't.

I have very fair skin, like my China doll. I named her Meg, after the character in *Little Women*. She has a metal hole in her back, under her dress. You can wind her up with a key and she'll play a song. *Try to remember the kind of September when you were a young and callow fellow.* She is a child-size music box, her hair in ringlets, her dress a silky pinafore. She wears pantaloons under her dress, a lacy collar up to her chin, her arms completely covered. I want to live back in time, want to cover my entire body in fabric so no one can see what's wrong with me. Surely there must be something wrong with me. At lunch yesterday, Jimmy Carter said that if you masturbate, you'll grow hair on the palms of your hands, and anyone who looks at you will know what you've done. I sit there, at a brown lunch table with rainbow-colored bench seats attached, trying not to look at my hands, afraid of what I might find.

There are different kinds of kids in Connellsville. There are mountain kids and city kids, band kids and chorus kids, bus kids and walker kids, Catholic kids and Protestant kids, welfare kids and middle-class kids, the preps and the scurfs, the smart kids, the Vo-Tech kids. We are defined by the things we do, the houses we live in, the jobs our parents work, the food we eat, the sports we play, the shoes we wear.

The most important rivalry is between the glass kids and the cap kids. The glass kids are children whose parents work in the glass factory, making bottles and jars and jugs to be shipped around the country, filled with beer or mustard or vinegar. The cap kids are children whose parents work at the factory next door, making corks and lids, bottle caps and other seals for the glass containers. The glass factory is hot, dirty, noisy: full of machines that can slice fingers; scaffolding that can collapse; furnaces that can ignite, starting underground fires. The cap factory is quiet, cleaner. There are no dangers there.

My parents make the vessels, the ships you can pour anything into. A cap is nothing without a bottle, a jar useless without a lid. In the chicken or egg discussion of container making, it's the glass that comes first, rolling warm from metallic lines, out of the smoky furnace. The glass is the first creation. It must be there, must exist before it can be filled with things that can feed you, quench your thirst, make your baby stop crying, make you drunk. Even the thickest glass is transparent, filtering light like a prism when you hold it to the sun. Glass can make rainbows. You can look through glass to see the world outside. You can look through glass to see yourself.

★ ★ ★

It's October, and I'm a pirate for Halloween. I have a hat with a skull and crossbones on it, an eye patch, a red and white striped satin blouse. I have a plastic dagger with a retractable blade and giant gold hoop earrings, of which I wear just one. Samuel is a vampire. He wears a plastic cape that makes a rustling sound when he walks, and white powdery makeup I helped him with, red lipstick making a stain on his chin, impersonating blood. Sarah comes along, too, wearing a rainbow-colored clown suit, silky like my mother's nightgowns, her real hair hidden under a bright blue wig.

We set out for trick-or-treating, pillowcases for candy we collect piece by piece, house by house. Mr. Riley hands out apples, Mrs. Bernardo popcorn balls wrapped in stiff paper. They both land in our sacks with a thud. We only want chocolate, or Jolly Ranchers that shine like small jewels when we hold them up to the light.

We walk down streets named after presidents, or trees—Jefferson, Sycamore, Washington, Chestnut. Some sidewalks are flat and smooth, and our feet find their way easily. Others have shifted like tectonic plates, roots underground pushing everything around, angry veins without enough room to grow. We try not to trip on the concrete, try not to stray from the parade of other children walking with us, costumes glowing in different shades of green and red and blue in the near dark of the evening.

Samuel has a flashlight, but we don't turn it on. We just keep walking, keep knocking on doors that open, offering sweetness to three children who could be any children, really. Maybe we wish that we really were a pirate, a vampire, a clown. Maybe we wish that we were a mother, a father, a daughter.

That night, Samuel wakes up screaming. His parents run down the white hallway and into his room. Samuel says his back hurts, that he feels paralyzed, can barely move. His parents get dressed, then wake up Greg and Danny, who must take care of Sarah, as she is wide awake from all the commotion. Samuel is glued to his bed. He can't stop moaning. Greg and Danny are scared. Everyone is scared, except Sarah, who doesn't really know what's happening. Samuel's dad carries him down the creaky staircase, the familiar sound of stretching wood on step ten, step seven, step two. Somewhere, on the way down, Samuel stops breathing. He's gasping, his open mouth like a fish, used to breathing water, now stranded on land.

They drive Samuel to the hospital in town, and there, the doctors try to help him breathe. They want to thread a long tube down his throat, but there's something wrong. It won't work, even though it should. So they cut a hole in Samuel's neck, a hole for him to breathe through. Then they put him in a helicopter and fly him fifty miles away to Pittsburgh, to Children's Hospital, where he is hooked up to a machine that breathes for him, a ventilator that pumps like an accordion. I've seen this on shows like *Trapper John, M.D.* The ventilator makes a hissing noise as it breathes for you, a healing snake for your lungs. It's rhythmic. It can put you in a trance if you're not careful.

I've never been to Children's Hospital, but I've always wondered what it looks like inside. I imagine rows of kids under pastel blue blankets, hooked up to machines that hum, bundles of clear tubing curled at their feet, a paper chart on a metallic clipboard dangling next to each bed, the fate of each child represented by a chart, strange symbols in red ink.

Greg rings our doorbell that morning, tells my mother what has happened. I listen from the kitchen as he talks about Samuel. My mother gives him a hug, says, "Let us know when you hear more."

I go to the basement, click on the record player, watch the bare turntable spin, let my fingers touch the edge ever so slightly. I like the thin vibration. It comforts me. I don't want to hear any music right now. I just want to watch the turntable spin, dizzy myself from the spinning, until Samuel can breathe on his own again.

# CHAPTER 14

# You'll Cry after Eleven

My father was in the Army. He enlisted when he was twenty-five. He had basic training in Frankfort, Kentucky, although in my mind, I picture Fort Knox, where the US government keeps all their money—gold bars and piles and piles of heavy coins, stacks of hundred dollar bills fastened with paper bands, the smell of dirty currency that must be in the air there, that scent of worn metal, of oily skin mixed with ink, like reading the newspaper with sweaty hands, the way the letters rub off on your fingers.

Dad's teeth were rotten when he arrived for basic training, and an Army dentist pulled them all out except for four on the bottom. Just like the grainy footage of sheared men shoulder to shoulder, enduring an assembly line of vaccinations, I imagine my father walking a gauntlet of dental torture, each step another tooth pulled until his gums are bare and bleeding. Today, I watch him take his dentures out to clean them, scrub them with a hard red toothbrush. He runs them under the faucet, beneath mounds of Colgate foam.

We only use Colgate, the white paste variety, although I want to brush my teeth with blue or green gel, a sticky sweet concoction that will keep the cavity creeps away. Sometimes my mother uses Pearl Drops, a slick triangle-shaped tube just for her. On the label it says *tooth polish* not *toothpaste*. It is glamorous. On the Pearl Drops commercial, a woman runs her tongue over her front teeth, tasting them. They taste delicious, and she makes a noise that sounds like sex.

My father takes his teeth out only when he brushes them. He leaves them in at night, no glass of soaking dentures on his nightstand. He also doesn't use any adhesive to keep them in place, even when he eats corn on the cob in the summertime. He says it's because his teeth were made by the Army, designed by engineers who know how to fashion teeth so they will stay inside your mouth. I wish he needed Poligrip, so I could play with it. On the Poligrip commercial, a man glues a heavy coffee cup to his finger, holds it in the air, dangling. I keep waiting for the mug to drop and shatter, but it never does.

When I catch my father brushing his teeth, I beg him to smile. I want to see him mostly toothless, smooth pink gums like a baby's newborn mouth. In pre-Army snapshots of my father, he smiles with his mouth closed. Only one photo, taken just before he left for basic training, reveals his gray teeth, pointy and crooked. They look hollow. In the picture, he is wearing his uniform, standing in between his parents, one arm wrapped around his mother's shoulder, one arm wrapped around his father's shoulder.

My grandfather, Edison, looked like an elf. He had a small face, no teeth himself, slightly pointed ears, an impish smile that reminds me of Jack Frost—rosy cheeks, pink nose (also slightly pointed). My grandfather did two things in his life—worked in a coal mine and drank whiskey. My father remembers him coming home after work, filthy and dark, his face disappearing beneath all that coal and ash. Edison would turn on the radio and drink and dance around the kitchen, stumbling, falling over, and laughing. My father liked these times, looked forward to his father happy as a pig in slop as they say. It's what came later on those nights that he never talks about, and the days the children couldn't eat because my grandfather had drunk all the money, my grandmother begging the neighbors for an egg, a cup of flour, anything they could spare.

Sometimes, my father will flash me a quick smile, his mouth open for a just a second or so, his hands still scrubbing his Army teeth. He knows that I love this little treat, this little minute we share, him bent over the powder blue sink, me standing in the hallway, watching, writing it down in my mind, like a flashbulb memory, our own time capsule.

★ ★ ★

It's almost Christmas time. We are doing the things we always do, our small traditions, just the four of us, no one else allowed inside. We load ourselves into the Lincoln, Linda and me shivering in the cold vinyl backseat. We drive to the Christmas tree lot, only it's not like other lots, the kind you see in movies and on the side of the road. There are no handmade signs and strings of white lights. There is no salesman bundled under layers of hunting orange. This place is an indoor showroom, the kind they have for cars and trucks at dealerships, the vehicles inexplicably inside the building. Do they drive them inside? Take the roof off and lower them down with rope?

This showroom is full of white trees. They have been flocked, their branches covered in something that resembles the hard icing on a birthday cake. If you touch a branch, the white stuff crumbles, powder landing on the floor in clumps. The trees are dead, so they don't need water. I wonder if they are petrified, as I walk between trees of different sizes, lined up in rows, a pretend forest of bleach white.

I like words with more than one meaning. Petrified is an adjective that can mean *converted into a stony substance* or *frightened so as unable to think or move.* But there is a figurative meaning, too—*deprived of vitality or the capacity to change.* We are all petrified in our own ways. We will all end up as fossils, our shapes eventually pressed into the ground and hardened.

Each tree has been trimmed of its lowest branches, less mess, less fuss. These are designer trees, the only ones my mother wants. She doesn't want needles all over the floor. She's lost her sense of smell, so she isn't moved by the scent of fresh pine. She wants dead and white and clean. The tree trunks are glued to stands, wooden *X*'s that support the weight of each tree, the ornaments that my mother will place on every branch, all red, no other colors allowed. We have shiny red glass balls, little fat Santas in red suits, red velvet bows, red and white striped candy canes that we aren't allowed to eat until after New Year's Day.

My mother circles the different models, inspects each tree from the bottom up, finally selecting the right size and shape for our living room, the tree with the most flocking, the tree with the fullest body, nothing thin or frail. The tree must be hearty, even though it is dead and we won't have to water it. It must be perfect. It must make no sound. It must produce no aroma. It must be a blank sheet on which my mother will hang artificial apples.

I want a green tree, a living thing I can take care of. I want to decorate it with homemade strings of popcorn, want to prick my finger with the needle while we all laugh and drink eggnog. I want to open the door of our house and be greeted with the smell of pine, to feel like I'm in a forest. I want colored lights instead of white ones. I want a star on top instead of a bow.

Samuel is still in the hospital, in Pittsburgh. Kids at school ask me about him. They've heard about the kid in third grade who stopped breathing, the kid in the rumors. Some people say they heard he is going to die. They ask me for the truth and I tell them I don't know, but my mother says Samuel will come home soon.

Alicia comes over one afternoon. She and my mother sit in the dining room drinking General Foods International Coffee. My mother lets Alicia smoke inside our house, pulls out the Santa

Claus ashtray from what we call the attic way, a little door in the hall that leads to a crawlspace that leads to the attic. Our house is a body, connective tissue linking one part to another to another, pipes and hoses are veins, pumping air and water through the place like oxygen, like blood.

I'm in my bedroom with the door open, listening. All the doctors know is that some sort of bacteria attached itself to Samuel's spine and wouldn't let go. It grew and grew until it got so big, it interfered with the signals to Samuel's brain. That's why he couldn't move, and couldn't breathe. The bacteria paralyzed him, tried to suffocate him. Surely, it wished to kill him. The doctors don't know where the bacteria came from. This could have happened to anyone. This could have happened to anyone's child.

Samuel loves G.I. Joe. He wants *Rolling Thunder*, the plastic war tank covered in machine guns. Alicia says that when Samuel first got out of the ICU and could finally talk, he kept talking about *Rolling Thunder*. "He was delirious," she says. "He just kept repeating it, '*I want Rolling Thunder.*' Almost like he was having a bad dream."

My mother and I go to visit Samuel. I get to stay home from school, and we drive into Pittsburgh during morning rush hour, cars lining the Parkway East as far as I can see, the windshield foggy from our body heat, much warmer inside than outside. We listen to Neal Sedaka on 8-track the whole way. I know all the words, but don't sing, not even when my favorite, "Run Samson Run," comes on. I am no longer concerned that Delilah is on her way. She can shave Samson's head for all I care.

We arrive at the hospital, each corridor its own maze, columns of white, hallways of white. The whole place smells like the soap in the restrooms at school, the liquid pink we wash with under cold water before returning to class. We find Samuel's wing, nurses in bright colors huddled around the reception desk, stethoscopes around their necks. My mother lets me ask for him. My throat is dry, I am nervous. Does this mean I am in love with Samuel? Does this make me his girlfriend?

Once, at his house, when his parents weren't home, I spied on him changing into his swim trunks. He was in his bedroom, the door open slightly, my one eye squinting, face pressed to the crack of light. I saw white flesh, then the smooth pink of his small penis, and my heart beat wildly in my chest.

My mother and I are taken to a playroom, where sick children build with LEGOs, push trains across the carpet, brush the silky hair of a baby doll, and watch cartoons. Samuel is one of them, sitting at a bright green table and chairs, coloring. I linger in the doorway for a moment, worried he won't look up. I want to see him see me. After I run through every moment we ever spent together in my mind, Samuel turns his head, smiles. He looks a little sad, and now I'm afraid I've upset him. But he stands up and walks to me anyway. We don't hug or kiss or touch in any way, unfamiliar with greeting each other after such a long absence. It occurs to me now that we never say hello or goodbye, each day together just a continuation of the next, no need for landmarks, for beginnings and endings.

We don't talk much, just look at each other for a while, until my mother breaks what she thinks is awkward silence. She doesn't understand our language, the silence of friends. My mother has only had one friend in her life, a girl named Bonnie who grew up not far from Atlas Avenue. My mother and Bonnie were champions of jacks, a game I can't perfect no matter how many hours I spend with the small metal stars, the red rubber ball, the threesies and foursies. My mother keeps her own set in her dresser drawer, takes them out from time to time, tries without patience to teach me. But I am not Bonnie. I can't play jacks or walk to the lunch counter at Burns Drug Store and order a Cherry Coke with real cherry or watch double-feature matinees of romantic movies at the movie theater downtown.

Mother, I wasn't born to be your friend, your secret keeper, your partner in crime, although I sometimes wish it were true, that we really were built the same, assembled from the same factory, made from the same cloth of cells, formula of blood and bone, that I was the twin you absorbed in the womb, my soul somehow catching inside you, sleeping perfectly still until the day you gave birth to me, the sister you were supposed to have, your motherless daughter, here to soak up half of your pain, turn it into love if I can.

★ ★ ★

By Christmas morning, Samuel has been home from the hospital for a while, but I haven't seen too much of him yet, just a general idea of his presence returned to the world. He's been inside his house, healing. There is still a hole in this neck, a faint whistling sound coming from it when he breathes. He had a tracheotomy, which I look up in our Encyclopedia Britannica as soon as I overhear my mother talking about it on the phone. The doctors made a hole in the front of Samuel's neck called a stoma. They slid some sort of tube inside so he could breathe from it, instead of through his nose and mouth. He will probably have a scar.

I change out of my pajamas quickly, open my presents with little thought. My parents sit sleepily on the couch, rubbing their eyes, my mother pale without makeup. The Beach Boys Christmas album is playing on 8-track, wafting in from the kitchen counter. Right now the Beach Boys are singing about Santa's souped-up sleigh in their strange high-pitched voices. *Run run reindeer.* The Beach Boys have a fascination with fast cars and sleds and other automobiles.

As soon as Linda and I are finished tearing into Nintendo games and sweaters and lighted makeup mirrors that have different settings for day and evening, so you can apply your eye shadow with a heavy hand when getting ready for a night on the town, I run over to Samuel's house.

I ring the bell and wait on their front porch, the sleeves of my new Garfield sweatshirt pulled over my hands. I can hear their morning sounds, the television blaring a Christmas parade, Sarah banging on something she shouldn't. After a few minutes, Samuel comes to the door. He's ready to go, a wool scarf wrapped around his wounded neck as Alicia kisses him goodbye. I've never seen her kiss him before, figure it must be a side effect of his illness. "Be back by noon, okay?" she asks, but it's more of a statement, really. The screen door snaps shut and Samuel and I walk away. I usher him into the warmth of my house, ask to take his scarf. I am what I have always wanted to be—his hostess, his caregiver, the little voice in his ear that says "stay awhile."

My mother behaves as though a dying person has entered the room. Her face lights up in response to tragedy, however minor, and even though Samuel has recovered, even though you would hardly know that he stopped breathing that night after trick-or-treating, which was almost two months ago, my mother must smooth a spot for him on the couch, cover his lap with a blanket, ask if he would like some hot tea.

"He doesn't drink tea," I say. My mother looks flustered, her hands unable to still themselves, so she decides to excuse herself to the kitchen, where a turkey is roasting in the oven.

"Perhaps the bird needs a basting," my mother suggests. The strain in her voice makes Linda and my father scatter. He descends to the basement to watch TV. Linda scurries to her bedroom to call her girlfriends and find out which shades of nail polish and eye shadow they received for Christmas.

My mother disappears into the kitchen. We hear the oven door open, metal rack slide out. We hear the suction sound of the turkey baster collecting shiny oil, sucking it up like the long nose of a hummingbird. I wonder if this sound reminds Samuel of the hospital, the suction of blood, sucking sounds of machines that kept him alive.

I give Samuel his present, watch him unwrap the large box with anticipation. I convinced my mother to buy him Rolling Thunder, the G.I. Joe tank Alicia said he asked for when he was in the hospital. It's a serious gift. It's a gift for a child who almost died. I want to show him how much he means to me, hope that the gift will somehow say what I'm not able to.

"Let me take your picture," I say to him, and grab my camera. I finally got one with auto focus so entire rolls of film don't come out blurry anymore, no more disappointment as I leaf through stacks of foggy images at the drug store counter. "Sit in the chair, next to the Christmas tree." I need evidence of the holiday in the shot, need to remember that this was our last Christmas together. Next year I'll be in junior high and Samuel will stay in elementary school. We're three grades apart, so we'll never be in the same school building together again, will never walk home together again, stopping for orange pop at the corner, collecting leaves for me to press between dictionaries under my bed.

I need to remember this minute, Samuel's smile, his incredibly blond hair, the little splash of freckles across his cheeks. I need to remember because I already know things will never be the same, that rattle of his almost death between us now, as though it made us feel too much, made us self-conscious about playing house all this time. I am not his child bride. Samuel smiles. The camera clicks. The sandbox is empty now, softly packed with snow. We won't notice when it melts.

# CHAPTER 15

# Knock on Wood

It's 1989 and everything is burning. Billy Joel wails from the white miniature television set in my bedroom, a futuristic kitchen in flames around him. Students stare down tanks in Tiananmen Square. Rescue workers rub oil from ducks after gallons bleed from the *Exxon Valdez,* their blue-gloved hands lost beneath foaming mounds of dish soap. Men and women hold handmade signs outside a Florida correctional facility, cheering the execution of serial killer Ted Bundy, a man my mother judges too handsome to be a murderer. One sign, in chunky block letters, reads HAVE A SEAT TED. In my mind, Ted's scalp sizzles as smoke from the electric chair smolders.

All this burning feels like chaos, not the controlled burn I long for, like the rusted barrel our neighbor sparks trash in, on Thursdays. We have to close every window to escape tiny flecks of cinder and ash that waft across the alley, to our red brick home. I am twelve for most of 1989, having been a late November child, a fact that makes me naturally smarter than others, insists my mother, who believes children born in the summer are disadvantaged. Sweltering heat makes part of a baby's brain melt, while cold air is good for the brain.

I think about a movie I watched on TV about a baby trapped in a well in Texas. Her name is Jessica and she doesn't need a last name anymore. She is "Baby Jessica" now as if she will always be a baby. As if Baby has become her first name, Jessica her last name. I remember watching the news coverage about her two years ago on CNN, a new channel that shows news twenty-four hours a day instead of signing off at midnight the way some TV stations used to do. They would play "The Star Spangled Banner," and then the screen would turn to static, that black-and-white fuzzy picture that Carol Anne spoke to in the movie *Poltergeist*. I don't like horror movies, but I told myself I had to watch that movie or else I would be the next little girl to get sucked up by the spirit world.

My mother's family ghosts seem friendly to her, but I'm not so sure. She thinks it's good for spirits to visit you, thinks it's more of a function of the dead needing to tell you everything's okay, or to remind you of something.

My mother feels her dead parents' spirits every time she tries to forget about them. She becomes difficult for weeks, even months surrounding their birthdays and their death days, so between her mother, her father, her grandmother Lindermann, and her two dead brothers, there is a lot of feeling and remembering to do. And it's hard work, it really is. I try to keep up with it all, make myself available for comfort. Sometimes my mother comes into my room at night and she crawls in bed with me. I let her do what she needs to do because it makes her feel better. I can only do so much, but I can do that. She can use me. Isn't that what a child is for?

The old joke goes something like this: "When they were passing out brains, you thought they said trains and you jumped on." I think some people are born missing certain parts. Not parts as obvious as brains of course, but small things, tiny fractures in the soul of a person that can't be repaired. The plumbing works even when there's a leak in one of the pipes, and you have to keep a bucket under the sink to collect water droplets that bead up on the surface, then drip down. You don't notice it at first, but over time the bucket fills to the rim, so you empty it and this becomes your routine. It seems like a minor annoyance, but if you add up every minute you spend empty-ing the bucket, it accumulates until you realize you've spent one-fifth of your life emptying buckets.

I'm intrigued by those books that tell you how long you spend doing certain things over the course of your life, like standing in lines for three years, or sleeping for twenty-two. Somehow we can't feel the measure of time as it's passing, don't notice how many min-utes we spend brushing our teeth while we're in the moment, so we need someone to calculate it for us. It's the accumulation that gets you. Living with my mother is like living with that bucket slowly filling under the sink. You remember that it's there, even when you can't see it, even when you try to forget. You know it will be waiting for you to empty, over and over again.

★ ★ ★

It's almost Valentine's Day and I have my period for the first time. It happened just as I was getting ready to leave for All-Star Chorus practice. I'd been playing a Summer Olympics computer game on the Commodore in the basement, and even though my mother had been yelling down the stairs for me to hurry up and get ready, I was trying to beat my high score in platform diving. My mother's voice kept tumbling down the stairwell toward me, first slowly, then faster and faster, my first name and middle name spoken together to indi-cate that she meant business. I finally gave in and dashed up to the bathroom to pee before we left.

I was just sitting on the toilet thinking about what exactly? I was thinking about nothing, actually. That's how simple life seemed in those minutes before I looked at the white panties stretched between my knees, before I saw the truth of what was happening. The blood had felt like nothing coming out. Like air, like light, nothing at all. What would have happened if I'd never looked down?

I'm finding it difficult to concentrate on the alto part for "Hello Again." At All-Star Chorus practice, we're working on a medley of Neil Diamond's ballads that also includes "You Don't Bring Me Flowers" and "Song Sung Blue." It's a combined chorus of fifth and sixth graders from all the elementary schools in the district. I sit next to Jamie Costello, a fifth grader with a perfect olive complexion and silky light brown hair. She doesn't talk to me much, except for the time I had a giant pimple right above my lip. Of course, she asked if it was a cold sore, which was just a way of drawing attention to something I apparently had no control over.

As if the question itself wasn't bad enough, my answer was even worse. I really didn't want her to think I had a cold sore, but I also didn't want her to know it was a pimple. I said, "I don't know what it is, but I think I got it from my cat. She's always sniffing my lips." Okay, great. What's worse than herpes and pimples? Some mysterious disease contracted from kissing your cat. And why are you kissing your cat anyway? It was a disaster. She spoke to me even less after that.

I've made it through the two-hour rehearsal without shifting my weight or getting up during break time. I'm afraid to move, unsure how the maxi pad between my legs will react. It's finally pickup time, and I stand, hoping that no one is watching me from behind. I climb into the Blazer, my father at the wheel, the heater ticking warm air on my face. The Pittsburgh Penguins hockey game is being called on the crinkled waves of the AM radio, its display lit up like a mouth on fire. "We're winning, 3 to 1," my father reports, sliding the smooth metal arm of the heater's control panel to turn it down a notch.

I nod and smile and stare out the side window at the darkened landscape on the ten-minute drive home—bony trees, flowerless rhododendrons, living room windows glowing warm and inviting in the cool winter air. *What will happen if I open the door and roll out?* I've seen MacGyver do it a dozen times. He tucks himself into a human cylinder, bracing himself against a dirt road. But this is asphalt. I don't think I could pull it off. So I'm going to have to tell my mother about getting my period.

When we arrive home, I find her sitting at the dining room table, wearing her gold-rimmed reading glasses, her small box with the blue flowers opened to reveal all her bill-paying accessories: checkbook, silver refillable pen that belonged to my grandfather, brown accordion folder for receipts, stamps. She's drinking a cup of Suisse Mocha, her favorite flavor of General Food International Coffees. I'd microwaved myself a cup once, when she and my dad were in bed for the night, but it didn't taste the way I'd wanted it to. Still, I huddled over it in my room while reading Stephen King's *Carrie*. I was stuck on a line where Chris, one of Carrie's female tormentors describes the feeling of losing her virginity as being *reamed out with a hoe handle.* This sensation, I thought, I could certainly do without. I plop myself down on one of the dining room chairs, its latticework scratching my back through my sweatshirt.

I sit perfectly still, willing my mother to notice me, like the nights I hover over her sleeping form trying to wake her up with my mind. Stephen King's Carrie became telekinetic after she started her period. In the scene where the girls in the locker room pelt her with tampons and maxi pads, a light flickers overhead. I watch the dining room chandelier for changes.

"What is it?" my mother asks. There is an edge to her voice that means my sitting there is making her nervous. She doesn't like children close to her and that is her standard reasoning: *You're making me nervous.*

"I think I got my period today." My voice sounds much squeakier than I remember, breaking slightly at the end like Peter Brady in the famous "Time to Change" episode of *The Brady Bunch*.

She licks an envelope flap and folds it over, its blue cross-hatched security lining flashing. I feel like taking an exaggerated gulp the way they do in cartoons, waiting at the edge of the newly re-upholstered chair. Mother recently changed our home's color scheme from orange and brown to green and gold.

"Well, you're twelve years old," she declares. "So I knew it would happen soon. I was twelve years old, Pam was twelve years old, Linda was twelve years old." Her voice trails off. She is trying to tell me how inconsequential my news is, that she can't be bothered with the business of my growing up.

In the book, Carrie's mother hadn't told her anything about menstruation. Carrie was scared that day after gym class when she started bleeding. She thought she'd hurt herself. She was never the same after that day, staring at a small puddle of her own blood, her mother at home with all the curtains drawn, a makeshift altar on the mantel.

There is no hugging, no taking me in her arms, no tears at the news of this event. I know where the maxi pads are kept, always have. Not because my mother showed me, but because I like to snoop around under the bathroom sink, and that's where they live in their soft blue wrappings.

In Judy Blume books when a character gets her period, there is fanfare of some sort—a mother says how proud she is of her girl, an older sister gives advice, a best friend compares notes on the telephone late into the night. There will be none of that for me. I'll take care of myself alone, only the words of the girl who played *Annie* on Broadway to comfort me.

I want to go back to that day in the school library, a room full of girls sitting at smooth green tables, the shades drawn so we could see the images of our future. I want to jump into those scenes with the girl who played *Annie* on Broadway, the way Mary Poppins and Bert the chimney sweep and Jane and Michael Banks jumped into the sidewalk drawings in *Mary Poppins*. The girl who played *Annie* on Broadway will take me to live with her and the other orphans and we'll dance and sing "It's the Hard Knock Life" and we'll all be okay in the end.

# CHAPTER 16

# Dogs Howling in the Dark of Night

It's springtime, and sixth grade is almost over. Soon I will leave the elementary school and enter junior high, where I'll put my books in a locker and be forced to take showers after gym class. (The creepy female gym teachers will stand in the locker room and watch and they'll justify it by saying they have to make sure all the girls practice good hygiene.) I'll learn how to make a pillow with a sewing machine in home ec and shred the tip of my right thumb on the jigsaw in wood shop. I want to get away from Heather Grain and I'm pretty sure I will. She'll be in the middle-track classes and I'll be in top tier, but her house is just a few blocks from ours, so I'll have to see her on the bus twice a day.

One morning, a boy on the bus will have a magazine page he's ripped from his dad's *Hustler*. It will show a woman on her knees, naked, a triangle of ash-blond pubic hair between her legs. She will be straddling a man's face, his mouth and nose inside of her. *He's eating her out*, the boy will say, and I will laugh a small nervous laugh because I'll like looking at the picture and hearing the boy talk about it and I'll want him to talk about it some more.

But my laugh will make Heather Grain notice me and that will be a mistake. She will turn to me, her green eyes drilling holes into mine. "No one will ever eat you out because your pussy is so hairy even you can't find it." She'll say this as if I'm invisible, not even there. She'll say this as if she's able to read my mind.

The summer before junior high I begin to feel a sense of doom washing over me, a river of doom perceptible only to me. I count everything I can get my hands on, repeat silent mantras in my head, wish on every eyelash, every North Star, every puff of dandelion seed I explode with my breath. The seeds break and hover in the air, tiny clouds of plant-based smoke.

I work to keep myself barely visible around the house. I don't like to get in my mother's way. She appears to be far far away, as if I'm looking at her through the wrong end of a pair of binoculars, as if she exists in a little glass globe up high on a shelf. Linda is going to be in high school in the fall, and my mother has turned most of her energy to editing and critiquing Linda's social life.

Mother doesn't like Linda's friends. Jenny Marcus is an airhead, Krista Clay is rude, Mary Margaret Pearson is too skinny and her family is cheap (a bunch of skinflints). Heather Ohler's little brother has diabetes, which isn't contagious, but still, my mother doesn't want Linda spending the night at their house just in case. Joelle Stockman is arrogant and wears too much eye makeup.

Rochelle's family moved to California last year. My mother liked them because they were considered wealthy for Connellsville. They had white carpet all over their home and they had a maid, but Rochelle's father got transferred at his job doing I don't know what. Another family is living in their house now, and it seems strange to think of other girls hanging out in Rochelle's basement, watching *Dirty Dancing* and talking about Patrick Swayze's ass in those tight black pants.

In spite of Joelle Stockman's fondness for electric blue mascara, my mother is letting her have her birthday party in our swimming pool. Joelle's mother, Maggie, is divorced. She's wears bright pink lipstick and has a boyfriend named Gallo who is rumored to be involved in shady business dealings around town. Joelle and Maggie live in the same apartment complex my grandfather died in. One would think this is a creepy connection, but my mother is thrilled with it, reminding me of the fact every time Joelle's name is mentioned around our house.

Joelle and Maggie arrive at our back gate, their car filled with a cake and decorations and some presents. Linda opens the back gate for them so they can park in our driveway. Teenagers start arriving, and music plays from Linda's yellow Memorex boom box, scratchy dispatches from B94 FM, our favorite radio station, broadcast from Pittsburgh. Boys are doing cannonballs from the diving board, staging biggest splash contests. Girls are milling around the pool, not wanting to get their hair wet just yet, adjusting their bathing suits around the areas on their bodies where stray pubic hairs might creep out. Even the girls who are naturally blonde have darker hair down there, and I feel like a pervert because that's what I'm most interested in looking at, along with their hard nipples popping up under bikini tops. The pool water is cold.

I'm on the back porch, just watching the show, when I hear a *whack*, like the muffled sound of the teacher giving Jimmy Carter a crack in the hallway. Then I hear a dog squealing, so I look for Honey Louise, then see her running fast through the open gate, into the driveway. I run down the back porch steps to greet her somewhere in the middle of the driveway, leaning down to pet her tangled beige fur. It strikes me now that she is the color of honey herself, and she's sweet, the right name for the dog.

I think about how much naming matters, even though most of us don't choose our own names. The power of naming things hits me like a blunt object over my head. The power of naming things, the power of words, bludgeons me at this moment, as I run my hand along Honey Louise's side, and it comes back smeared red with blood.

The squealing was the dog's pain. My father runs down the alley to investigate, and I'm worried for him. What if someone wants to hurt him, too? After what feels like forever, but is probably only about five minutes, my father returns with the report. Three boys were hanging out on a corner two blocks down Washington Avenue. They had a pellet gun. Maybe they shot Honey Louise on purpose. Maybe it was an accident. We won't find out because the boys ran when my father approached them. I try to imagine my father confronting them, but it's difficult to see him putting himself on the line like that, even though I know he loves this dog enough to do it.

The party guests are beginning to realize that something is happening. They can hear some commotion over their music and splashing. I run to get my mother from inside the house. She is making herself scarce on purpose, in silent protest of this party for a girl of which she doesn't entirely approve. She is making herself invisible, something I realize now that she's taught me to do, too. Maybe we are built the same. Maybe there was something different about me, the child born on the Sabbath. The little friend from the womb arriving to rescue her mother. Maybe I am some kind of Jesus.

Linda is upset. Most of the girls are in tears with her. Joelle feels worst of all, for it was she and her mother who forgot to close the back gate after they arrived. It was she and her mother who supplied the opening through which Honey Louise escaped.

I find my mother in her bedroom, lying sideways across the neatly made bed. She has all the blinds drawn, blocking out the sunlight. She's wearing jeans and a thin cotton blouse. She never wears shorts or skirts, even in the heat of summer. She's ashamed of her varicose veins, which are severe and bulging from years of standing on concrete at the factory, measuring the openings of baby food jars, making marks on them with a red grease pencil. Her work is called SQC, which stands for Selector Quality Control. The other workers on the line are simply called selectors, their job to watch the glass as it moves along lines. My mother is the one who inspects the vessels as they come off the line.

She looks for defects, abnormalities in the quality of the product. She communicates the measurements to the men working at the furnaces, tells them if they need to adjust their glass making. It's not glassblowing, it's not creative like that, although I've often pictured my father rolling a long metal rod between his thumbs, firing something liquid and beautiful into shape, something that resembles a cat's eye marble.

It's a Sunday, so my mother can't do any housework today. That is bad luck, and it's against God's wishes, which she abides even though we are not particularly religious. She does take Linda and me to Albright United Methodist church from time to time, but it's more of a social visit, not for worship. My mother likes that church because it's a block from the peeling yellow house on Atlas Avenue where she grew up, and many of the churchgoers remember her dead parents and dead brothers. They pat her arm and tell her how young she looks. They tell her they can't believe she works in a factory, she looks too glamorous for that. They tell her I look just like Pearl, my dead grandmother.

I'm shaking, but not crying. My eyes see things in slow motion, like one of our home movie reels when I place my hand on the film to slow to down. The images look choppy, blurred. My mother sits up. A puppy excited by the smell of bad news in the air. "Someone shot Honey Louise," I tell her. I feel like I'm in a soap opera, remembering watching *Dallas* years ago, all the headlines that summer asking, "Who shot J.R.?"

"Where is she?" my mother asks, still not standing, still not wanting to attend the party that's happening in our backyard, the thin boys with their mostly hairless chests and knobby knees, the chunky boys with their floppy breasts that look like mine.

My father has brought Honey Louise into my bedroom. She's resting on my bed on her good side, the side that doesn't have a metal diabolo pellet in it. Her breathing is shallow, but steady. Her black eyes are moist and dim. Since it's Sunday, the vet, Dr. Meerhoff, is out of town. My father talked to him on the phone, via his emergency number. Dr. Meerhoff instructed my father on how to stop the bleeding. He said the pellet will actually keep things in place for now. He says to let Honey Louise rest in a quiet room until he can make it back to Mt. Pleasant Animal Hospital, around 6:00 p.m. We can drive Honey Louise in then, my dad's Chevy Blazer becoming a dog ambulance.

We turn off all the lights in my bedroom and draw the blinds. I decide I'll stay with Honey Louise until it's time to go. I'll lay behind her, curving my body against hers. I have a dishtowel nearby in case of more bleeding, which the doctor says shouldn't come. I don't want to watch TV. I don't want to make any noises to disturb Honey Louise, so I grab a copy of Judy Blume's *Just as Long as We're Together*, begin to reread it silently. My mother, after inspecting my makeshift dog hospital, goes back to her room, closes the door this time. She won't emerge until after anything is over—the party, the trip to Dr. Meerhoff's, the cleaning up around the pool deck. She won't emerge even late into the night, when Honey Louise is back home again, stitched and wrapped in sterile gauze, eating ground deer meat from my father's palm.

On *Dallas*, it turned out to be Kristen who shot J. R. Ewing. She was his mistress, a word people only seem to use on TV. She shot J. R. in a fit of anger, but he eventually forgave her. I can't imagine forgiving the boys who did this to Honey Louise. I want something bad to happen to them in return. Every time Honey Louise sighs, I imagine something being taken from the boys. I start at the ends, first a finger, then another, then the toes. The sighs keep rolling from Honey Louise's fat black nose, so I move farther up the boys' bodies, cutting arms off at the elbows, legs at the knee, until eventually there's nothing left of them to take away.

## CHAPTER 17

# Howl for Death before Daylight

I am a cheerleader in seventh grade, although I am stuck on the second-rate "white squad" instead of the more prestigious "blue squad." Blue squad is for girls with the highest tryout scores. White squad is for girls who barely made it. Tryouts were held at the end of sixth grade, and Dina Corliss and I practiced our moves after school. Dina lives in South Connellsville, not far from the factory, and we'd both start walking from our own houses, usually meeting in the middle near the ball diamond on Austin Avenue. There, we'd pump MC Hammer from a battery-operated cassette player, dance to "U Can't Touch This" until our toe touches were almost high enough to be called toe touches, instead of lazy-looking, half-hearted *v* leaps.

Dina made the blue squad, and I made the white squad. I'm not very good at making my movements stiff and choppy. In cheerleading you have to clap as though there is a rubber band connecting your hands, and you can barely pull them apart before they snap back together. It's all about right angles and sharp poses. My body is too fluid, my arms and legs too limber from years of dance class.

Being a cheerleader sounds like a good way to start junior high. I get to wear the uniform to school on game days, my thighs sticking to the smooth wood grain of my seat in homeroom. I run for student council representative but am beaten by a boy named Jeremi, spelled with an *i* at the end. It's just a popularity contest, I know, but some kids don't seem to do anything to be popular. They just *are*, as if they are born with something extra, some ability to draw others in. I've been studying these people since kindergarten. They take different forms, so they are difficult to spot at first. They don't always look the same. Some are rich and some are poor. Some make really bad grades. Some pick their noses when they think nobody's looking. Some are seen at the grocery store with their parents.

Most of them don't even know my name, but I watch them anyway. I probably know the name of every kid in my grade, even though most of them wouldn't even recognize me if they saw me at Pizza Hut or down at the drug store. Or maybe they do recognize me—they just refuse to acknowledge me. It seems like it pains them to do so. I am that inferior and they need me to know that, to really understand that I mean nothing.

Amy Nickels and I don't have a single class together in seventh grade, but we see each other on the bus and eat lunch together. Now that we're in junior high, Amy's been reunited with her two cousins, who went to different elementary schools. The three of them are electricity when they're together. They share a language I find hard to comprehend. And they are turning bad, not rotten, but slightly spoiled, like cheese that's been left out of the refrigerator and has hardened just a bit. Yes, you can still eat it, and it still tastes like cheese for the most part, but something's changed, and other than the texture you can't quite put your finger on it.

I feel us being poured through a sieve, Amy and I, and somehow she is moving through. She is slippery, like oil, while I am caught at the bottom of the metal basin, forced to watch her through the holes.

I'm watching a movie of life and everyone has a role except me. That makes me the observer. I begin to feel convinced that I have been put on Earth for just this purpose. My actions have no meaning unless someone is there to witness them, and they rarely are. Even Linda, who is in high school now, doesn't seem to notice me even as we bump against each other down the hallway that connects our bedrooms, our sleeping patterns no longer in sync as they once were. I know I'm not disappearing, for I can still see myself in mirrors, and my mother has enough of them scattered all over the house, a reminder that I am still here. I'm not sure which is worse—wondering if you're invisible or knowing that you're not.

In junior high, you must claim people. They belong to you. They are yours. But I have no one to call my own. I'm still in IMPACT, but it's different in junior high, not as fun. Here, the IMPACT teacher is Mr. Rudd, a laid-back *Miami Vice* type who really doesn't care what we are up to. *Self Directed Study* is what he calls it. I use my time in class to research and write fan letters to my favorite famous people: Fred Savage, Greg Louganis, and Cher, among others. In some cases, they send me things in return, like an autographed photo of Greg executing a perfect pike position before he dives into the water.

In between classes, I walk the halls alone, while other girls run in packs like wolves, shouting and laughing and spraying alcohol into their mouths from re-purposed travel-size hairspray bottles. They smoke cigarettes in the bathrooms, blowing rings into the air, already thick with Charlie cologne or Exclamation perfume. I look at myself in the bathroom mirror while I wash my hands with cold water. I know every pore, every angle, every shadow on my face, from hours of studying myself in the mirrors at home.

Our house is full of mirrors, so it's difficult to avoid the way I look. In the dining room, my mother's hutch takes up an entire wall, the giant mirror in the middle flanked by mirrored cabinets on either side. This is where she keeps her *good dishes,* a collection of ugly white plates with dull gold-etched designs that look like they were drawn with a Spirograph. There is a large mural-sized mirror above the couch in the living room, surrounded by a chunky gold-toned frame that looks like it came from ancient Greece, a la *Clash of the Titans*.

I always felt sorry for poor Medusa, exiled to the Isle of the Dead. As if a head teeming with writhing snakes isn't horrible enough, she turns anyone she gazes upon into stone. Medusa used to be a beautiful woman until she fell in love with Poseidon. Aphrodite wanted Poseidon all to herself, so she turned Medusa into a monster. Her ability to fall in love became Medusa's fatal flaw. Every character needs a fatal flaw.

I close my parents' bedroom door, which has a full-length mirror tacked on the outside, and try on endless outfits, turning the hallway into my own runway. I like it best when I'm home alone, which is beginning to happen more and more as I get older, my parents still working swing shifts and sleeping a lot and Linda out with Christopher, her boyfriend who is a senior and has a Charlie Chaplin–esque mustache, which he is constantly touching to make sure it's still there, as if it might fall off or run away at any moment.

When I have an hour home alone, I make my rounds. First, I go into Linda's room and check out her underwear drawer. This is where she keeps intricately folded love notes from Christopher riddled with misspellings and grammatical errors. She also has a matching bra and panty set—it's bright teal and made of a satiny material. I try it on and dance around in front of the mirror, pretending that there are boys peeping at me through the window.

My next stop is my parents' nightstand drawer, which is a bit tame but still interesting. There I find my father's twenty-year watch from the factory—gold and still brand new in the blue velvet box that opens with a creak, like the jaws of a small clam. I also find old pictures of the two of them on their honeymoon—a camping trip in Maryland—and a half-empty jar of Vaseline.

Then I check in my parents' closet, my favorite spot. On the right, which is my father's side, there's a brown accordion envelope filled with real estate papers and our birth certificates. On the left, which is my mother's side, there is a shoebox with feathery open-toed pumps inside. I slide my feet into them and they fit. They are bedroom slippers, like the ones I've seen Doris Day wear in old movies. Doris is one of my mother's favorite actresses. She especially loves *Pillow Talk* co-starring Rock Hudson. Mother was crushed in 1985, when Rock died and the world learned that he was a gay man with AIDS.

"But he was a leading man," she says. "And so handsome." My mother doesn't like it when façades are shattered. When you've built your life around the premise that it's what's on the outside that counts, you don't appreciate being faced with the truth about insides. The truth about insides is that they always find a way of oozing through to the outside.

★ ★ ★

I never got to witness my mother being a daughter. She is an orphan in my mind, as if she sprung whole from some mysterious well, already formed. I can't image her sitting in her mother's lap as a child, or her father bandaging a skinned knee, rubbing alcohol on her skin and then blowing gently. Her parents are ghosts, and she misses them terribly. How can you miss someone so much when all they have given you is sadness? How can you lie in bed motionless on the anniversaries of their deaths, your breathing raw and shallow? I've started feeling embarrassed being seen in public with my mother, and when I act this way, my mother says, "You should feel lucky that I'm still alive. I would give anything to be able to go somewhere with my mother!"

My mother is investing in me, sure that I'll be famous one day. She changes her mind often regarding what I'll become famous for. Sometimes it's dancing, sometimes acting, sometimes the first female president of the United States, sometimes a powerful corporate executive, and sometimes the wife of a billionaire. She doesn't let me forget about Donald Trump's son, who is around my age. "Someday you can bump into him on purpose and tell him that when you were a little girl, your mother found out about him and said you should grow up and marry him. He'll think it's the cutest story. Maybe he'll even name a building after you."

Marrying well is an idea my mother has been drilling into me from birth. "Don't do what I did. Don't give your life away to a factory." She always quotes the old country song about manual labor by Hoyt Axton, "Boney Fingers": *Work your fingers to the bone and whaddya get? Boney fingers!* My father prefers the song "Sixteen Tons" to convey his feelings about factory work. He'll shuffle across the checkered kitchen linoleum while packing his lunch in the afternoon, singing *you load sixteen tons, whaddya get? Another day older and deeper in debt.*

My mother envies women who dress up for work, so we admire bank tellers, receptionists, and department store clerks. "Don't ever work a job where you get dirty," she says. Her work jeans were forever stained, oil permanently pressed into the seams. She has a collection of T-shirts in various stages of raggedness, which she wears in rotation. She cuts her own V-necks into the collars of the shirts, to allow more room to breathe.

Despite the filthiness of her work clothes, she never leaves the house without her T-shirt tucked in and her hair expertly teased and sprayed. She used aerosol Adorn for years until I finally guilted her into switching to pump hairspray after learning about CFCs and how they are eating away at the ozone layer. My mother is beautiful, with her platinum-blond hair and rouged cheeks. She is a movie star in work clothes. She smiles for the mirror, invisible flashbulbs popping down the hallway.

★ ★ ★

It's the first week of eighth grade and I'm sitting in homeroom with twenty other kids, waiting to be called to the auditorium for school yearbook photos. I had the horrible idea of getting a haircut and perm last weekend, thought getting rid of straight hair down to my waist would be good for my image. Instead, I look like a poodle with a chemical burn. Two of the cutest boys in eighth grade are in my homeroom this year: Jeremi with an *i* and Bryan with a *y*.

If you give a thirteen-year-old boy enough time to examine you, he'll think of something to tease you about. In this case, I might as well have been wearing a target around my neck, or a flashing neon sign pointing to my hair. Jeremi with an *i* and Bryan with a *y* don't waste much time.

"What happened to your hair?" It's Jeremi with an *i*.

"I got a perm." If I try hard enough, maybe I'll turn into one of the computers that line the walls. I am furniture, a piece of equipment, made to blend in or be used.

"So is that what your pubes look like?" It's Bryan with a *y* now. I hear a bomb explode when he says *pubes*. If you utter that word in a room full of eighth graders, they're listening. Whispers scurry along the baseboards, across the speckled terrazzo flooring, float in the air around our wooden graffiti covered desks.

I squirm in my seat for a minute, then look straight ahead like a good machine. I stare at the blackboard, where our homeroom teacher, Mr. Renaldo, stands preparing for his first period class, writing some basic computer programming on the board. It's code I learned five years ago in IMPACT. Mr. R., as he instructs students to call him, has a quiet, strange voice, froggy and mechanical.

"What's going on, people?" he turns around to ask, a dusty nub of yellow chalk in one hand, fluorescent light from the ceiling bouncing off his round glasses, making his eyes disappear.

The room straightens itself up, the kids all shutting up and pretending to look in their notebooks, at their shoes, trying to find a focal point to control their uncontrollable laughter. Bryan with a *y* and Jeremi with an *i* both put their heads on their desks, to muffle their laughter that sounds more and more like barking now, the boys becoming dogs. Suddenly I'm aware of the pennies in my shoes, the cherry Pop Tart from breakfast sitting in my stomach like a lump of clay. I make an executive decision. I need to change my image. I need to try to become popular. A lot of girls get popular by putting out, so that's what I'll do. I decide I should start with getting fingered. When a boy fingers a girl, *everyone* knows. Details emerge regarding the tightness or looseness of the girl's pussy, the way it smells, how wet she was, where it happened, whether or not the boy licked his fingers afterward. Dina Corliss says you have to let a boy break the seal sometime. To prove you're a woman. To prove you have something inside you worth taking.

★ ★ ★

I wear a gold guardian angel pin to school every day. My mother bought it for me at the Hallmark Store. It came pinned to a little card that explained how the angel looks after the person who wears it. I believe I have to wear it on the left side of my collar, the same side as my heart. I wear it for protection from *I don't know what*. When I think about the angel protecting me, I never say what I need protection from. If I do, it will become real, just like if I decide that aliens are real, they will hear me and abduct me, just to show me how real they are.

My mother smiles when she walks past my bedroom in the morning, sees me shining the little winged creature. The angel is naked except for a swatch of cloth slung around its hips. Once we were on our way to school in the car, almost there, in fact, when I realized I'd forgotten to pin my angel on to my blouse. I let out a loud "Oh!" and grabbed my chest, pleading with my mother to turn us around. I'd risk being tardy to make sure I had my angel with me for the day. This moment pleased my mother more than anything else I can remember. This moment made her proud.

★ ★ ★

In the world according to *Three's Company*, there are two kinds of women: Chrissies and Janets. You have to be one or the other. There seems to be no successful way to combine them. I am a Janet, the smarter, more sarcastic, darker-haired version, a foil to the blond and beautiful, big-breasted Chrissies of the world. But I will try to cross over. I could always bleach my hair. My mother does it once a month—two bottles of L'Oréal Preference and a pair of plastic gloves. It smells like a dead animal but my mother doesn't dare sit outside with gooey color on her head, so instead, she sits at the dining room table, clipping recipes from *Good Housekeeping*, sipping Sanka or hot water with lemon.

I've only seen one photo of my mother with dark hair. It was taken right after Linda was born, and my mother is holding her with a bewildered look on her face, a rare candid shot. My mother doesn't like candid photos. Every snapshot has to be planned, staged. You won't find any family pictures of us where we aren't posed like mannequins, uncomfortable smiles pasted onto our faces like we're made of paper and glue.

Why is it so easy for some girls, girls like Dina Corliss, who have full breasts and long straight hair and eyebrows that don't grow together like a caveman's? Why is it so difficult for me, with my less than A cup, my bad perm, my hairy upper lip, that shadowy mustache? Dina and I are becoming friends, getting closer and closer each day, and I like the way it feels to be wanted by her. Still, I know why she wants me—she wants an ugly friend to make her look even more gorgeous in comparison. She wants to always be the prettiest girl in the room.

All the boys have crushes on Dina, and I do, too. She seems to be made for desire. I'm only happy when I'm sharing oxygen with her, laying on the floor in her enormous bedroom listening to cassette singles on her Emerson stereo, making an infinite number of mixed tapes and coming up with nicknames for everyone in the eighth grade. Dina is still a cheerleader, still on the blue squad, while I quit cheerleading at the beginning of the year, having made the white squad for the second year in a row. I didn't want to be stuck on the squad with all the seventh graders. We were so terrible the only games we were assigned to cheer at were girls' basketball games. Girls cheering for girls. Everyone knows that's just unnatural.

My mother talks to Linda less and less, has begun shutting her out, first in small ways, then bigger ways. I wonder if that will ever happen to us, if she'll ever stop telling me hushed stories on her bed in the evenings. My father's bowel trouble seems to have gone away over the years, although we don't talk about it, just like we don't talk about 1985, that year the bubble burst over Connellsville and let evil in, slowly at first, but now it feels as though it's growing rapidly. We are just so goddamned vulnerable now, as Dina would say. Goddamned is Dina's favorite adjective, and to her, conversation just isn't conversation without it in every sentence.

I used to be afraid of saying bad words out loud, convinced something terrible would happen to me if I did, but Dina has taught me that cursing feels good. It feels like freedom pouring out of my mouth. We spend many hours in her basement, staying up all night playing video games while her parents sleep, cursing every pixel, every goddamned piece of shit obstacle that gets in our way, the pings and chimes of Super Mario Brothers egging us on. We don't clasp hands over our mouths or gasp or act shocked when we say bad words. We just open our mouths and let everything come out.

★ ★ ★

Three girls are huddled around a pink princess telephone, its padded numbers glowing as Dina, the unofficial leader of our group, dials. Every group needs an unofficial leader, and every girl needs a friend like Dina. We are listening to our favorite radio station on a yellow boom box, bedroom walls plastered with posters of movie stars and adorable animals, a girl's version of cave paintings. We are trying desperately to get through on the request line so we can ask them to play "She Blinded Me with Science." None of us can remember why we want to hear this song, but we are desperate just the same.

"Damn it Bobbi Jo, stop breathing! I can't hear myself think!" Dina says. She stands up to reach a stolen pack of her mother's Marlboros on the windowsill. Bobbi Jo stops breathing. The phone cord won't reach the windowsill, so I take over the dialing duties. I know I have permission, having been Dina's sidekick in training for months now, deliciously close to eclipsing Bobbi Jo, which is my secret goal. Every girl needs a secret goal.

Dina drags slowly on her cigarette, then blows smoke through the screen. We've locked ourselves in my bedroom, even though the house is empty. Linda is at her boyfriend's house and my parents are at my mother's high school reunion and they won't be home until very late and somehow they agreed to allow Dina and Bobbi Jo to spend the night. Bobbi Jo is Dina's friend, not mine, so we've developed that slightly competitive friend-of-a-friend relationship girls are known for. We have two things on our agenda tonight: smoke

Dina's mother's cigarettes and invite boys to come over. We've got the smoking part down. We're working on the boy part.

"Goddamn it, we need to get out of this room!" Dina screams. It's winter, and even though the window is open, the heater is pumping hot air through a tiny mouth in the wall, making the miniature room swelter. I hang up the phone while Dina snuffs out her cigarette in one of my mother's coffee cups we've filled with water. Bobbi Jo puts on some roll-on lip gloss that makes the whole room smell like strawberries.

It's freezing outside tonight, and Bobbi Jo wonders out loud if the cold will make the boys' dicks shrink, like when they get out of a swimming pool and you can see the outline of their little thingies inside their saturated trunks for just a second before they start adjusting, spoiling the view. Dina thinks that's the dumbest thing she's ever heard. Even dumber than the time Bobbi Jo thought you could get pregnant from a toilet seat.

"Seriously, though," Bobbi Jo explains. "What if you sit down to pee right after some guy jacks off on the seat?" Dina turns around and mouths the words *dumb ass* to me. I'm becoming addicted to these secret moments between us, but I'm working hard not to let it show.

"And who is this guy you share a toilet with who jacks off right before you go, anyway?" Dina asks, throwing her hands up in the air. She whips out a tiny brown compact and starts patting her nose and cheeks with pressed powder, as if she's about to call the boys via satellite. She coos our invitation into the receiver, her voice more like a bird's than a girl's, more song than syllable. She hangs up the phone. "They'll be here in twenty minutes."

Twenty minutes is an eternity in girl years, perhaps even longer. Dina gargles with a miniature bottle of green mouthwash, spitting the remains in the ash-filled coffee mug with a flourish. Then we head down to the basement to wait. The boys are Eric, Keith, and Kevin. I have a crush on Keith that nobody knows about. He's in IMPACT with me and we sat together on the bus during a field trip to the Buhl Planetarium in Pittsburgh this year. Every time the driver made a sudden stop, we lunged forward and yelled "Inertia!" then laughed our asses off.

Keith's favorite band is R.E.M., and his dark hair hangs in a natural flop over his right eye. His favorite video is "Losing My Religion." He has every one of Michael Stipe's movements memorized, which basically consists of pacing around an empty wooden room, jumping, wringing his hands, and looking thoughtful. All he needs is to hear the song and he can literally act out the video, like he's a human version of MTV.

When the doorbell rings, the three girls race around, literally running in circles for a moment, before regaining our composure and shooting *rock, paper, scissors* to determine which one of us must let in the boys. Bobbi Jo loses. "I fucking hate yinz," she moans as she pads up the shag carpet stairs. Here in southwestern Pennsylvania, we have our own vocabulary and accent. *Yinz* is what we say instead of the plural *you* or *you guys*. We also have a habit of leaving off the ending or beginning sounds of certain words. Window becomes *winda* and *that* becomes simply *at,* as in *Where'd at damn dog go?*

The basement stairs spit you out right at the front door, so Dina and I can hear the screen door close with a *ka-ching,* then the low rumbling of male voices. Bobbi Jo leads the parade of boys down the stairs and I catch a whiff of winter air and cologne—a mix of Polo and Drakkar. Eric is walking closely behind Bobbi Jo, threatening to goose her ass at any moment. She fake runs away, then grabs his hand and leads him to the couch, where they start kissing immediately.

Kevin slips his leather bomber jacket off and throws it at Dina. Underneath he's wearing a Dinosaur Jr. T-shirt and stonewashed jeans. It's 1991. Everything is stonewashed. The Dinosaur Jr. T-shirt is the same as the band's album cover, depicting a young girl standing on the beach with a cigarette dangling from her lips, her arms looking like thin straws and her dark hair looking stringy and dirty as it flaps in the wind. Keith takes off his green windbreaker, folds it neatly and places it gently on one corner of the couch.

Bobbi Jo and Eric are making out on the other corner of the couch, but the rest of us are just sitting there watching MTV.

"Let's play strip poker," Kevin says, but we're not falling for it.

"No way," Dina says. "That's just your excuse to see all of us naked."

"Okay, Mommy," Kevin says, adding "prude" under his breath. Prude is the highest insult in our school right now, having dethroned "scurf" months ago.

Since we're in my basement, it's my duty to steer the festivities in the right direction, so I turn up the volume on MTV, which is even more important to us than radio. Right now they're playing a Bryan Adams video, but I hope they'll play "Losing My Religion" soon. I just want to see Keith's brown eyes brighten a shade when he hears that mandolin, then Michael Stipe's vibrato come in. *Oh life, it's bigger, it's bigger than you and you are not me.*

"What the hell are those?" Kevin asks, pointing to my mother's collection of Elvis-shaped whiskey containers. They are carefully arranged on a giant plywood shelf my father built. They are difficult to miss. The display takes up an entire wall.

"They're for decoration," I say. "I mean, they have whiskey in them, but that's not why my mother collects them. She doesn't even drink. Plus, she says breaking the seal and drinking the whiskey makes them less valuable."

"Holy shit!" Eric says, breaking free from Bobbi Jo's suction on his neck. Bobbi Jo still thinks it's cool to give and receive hickeys, another aspect of her that grates on Dina's nerves. "Let's crack 'em open," he urges.

We all run over to the shelf to inspect the ceramic statues. Each represents a different point in The King's career, and plays a song to match. My mother has about twenty statues in all.

"Alright," I say, "but let's just pick one, okay?"

"How about this gold one?" Bobbi Jo offers.

"No, you idiot, that's probably the most important one!" Dina scolds.

"Yeah, Bobbi Jo, let's pick a less conspicuous one," I answer. Bobbi Jo is not the brightest of our bunch, and I know she has no idea what the word *conspicuous* means, which is precisely why I use it.

"Here, how about this one with the teddy bear?" Eric asks. "Aw, how cute. Elvis and his little stuffed bear," he teases, removing the miniature plush teddy from its place on Elvis's lap, rubbing it on Bobbi Jo's cheek.

"No, that's one of my mom's favorites," I inform him, swiping the bear from him.

"How about the army one?" Kevin asks. "The ceramic has a few chips in it anyway," he adds, inspecting the tiny flecks of white peeking through The King's dark coif of hair.

"Wait, this one probably has the most whiskey in it," Keith says with an adorably thoughtful look as he examines the centerpiece of my mother's collection: an ivory head and shoulders bust of Elvis engraved with his birth and death dates JANUARY 8, 1935 – AUGUST 16, 1977. With a finger, Keith traces Elvis's cheekbones, his empty eyes, and something resembling my heart skips a few beats in my chest as I realize I'll do anything he suggests.

The girls run upstairs to get the supplies: my mother's Tupperware tumblers, ice, a two-liter bottle of Coke. We love the idea of taking care of the boys, being domestic.

Elvis will become our new inside joke, and in school on Monday, we'll talk to each other in code, as in, *Wow, I really love Elvis, don't you?* We've emptied not only the ivory bust, but Blue Hawaii Elvis and Taking Care of Business Elvis. It turns out, each ceramic Elvis head is attached to a little cork that fits down into the cave of his neck. After pouring the amber liquid into our cups, we re-attach the paper seals with tiny dots of glue. Now the only way my mother will know is if she picks them up and notices the faint swooshing sound is gone.

"Alcohol evaporates anyway, so your mom won't think anything of it," Dina assures me, suddenly a liquids expert although science is her weakest subject. But nothing matters right now, as the six of us bask in the glow of Kentucky bourbon whiskey, which is what we're drinking, according to the gold-foil labels on the back of each Elvis.

"This is good shit," Eric says, taking another swig of his concoction. He leans in and gives Bobbi Jo what must be a whiskey-flavored kiss. The lights are out again, but MTV is still on, and the television is casting its blue glow on us. The boys are tipsier than the girls, with Eric bordering on falling-down drunk. Right now he's got Bobbi Jo pinned to the couch, writhing around on top of her like a snake while she pants softly.

MTV starts playing the video for "I Touch Myself" by The Divinyls. The lead singer, a sexy red-haired woman with bangs that cover her eyes, rolls around on the floor, singing. The boys start discussing masturbation. They all deny that they do it, of course. They want to know about us. The girls let out a collective *ewwwwww* as if touching our own bodies is filthy and gross. I wonder if Dina and Bobbi Jo are pretending like me. Pretending not to know and love the incredible feeling of making an orgasm.

I know the proper term for it now. I've looked it up in the dictionary. It can be a noun, as in the event of an orgasm, or it can be a verb, as in the action of reaching orgasm. The definition is *a climax of sexual excitement.* I imagine it as a pinnacle, the highest peak on a mountain. The word comes from the Greek *organ,* which means to swell or be excited. An organ is an instrument, a tool. A body is an instrument made up of smaller instruments. I am learning how to play my body, how to make it sing.

It's almost one in the morning, according to the small digital display on the VCR. "Shit!" I say as I peel myself off the couch, losing my balance slightly. "My parents will be home soon."

Getting three drunk teenage boys out of your house isn't easy. Bobbi Jo takes Eric to the garage for a hand job. "Watch out for whiskey dick!" Kevin warns, which is met with Eric's raised middle finger as he and Bobbi Jo disappear through the doorway. The TV is still tuned to MTV, but now *Headbangers Ball* is on, so the volume is on mute. A long-haired guitar-wielding man thrashes around a fake stage.

Keith and I begin playing a game of hot hands, and I'm on top. This means I place my hands, which are palms down, on his hands, which are palms up, and he tries to slap one (or both) of my hands before I can jerk them away. I'm only winning because his senses are a little more dulled than mine. I'm bolder from the alcohol, brave enough to suggest this excuse to touch Keith, to touch myself.

After a while, Bobbi Jo and Eric re-emerge and the caravan of boys begin their journey back to Kevin's house, where they're spending the night.

"We should do this again sometime," Dina says.

"Sure, just don't bring the ugly one next time," Kevin says back to her. He thinks he's whispering, but it's loud enough for everyone to hear. My face feels hot. I know he's talking about me. I know I'm the ugly one.

The girls say goodbye, the boys don't reply, just disappear into darkness, then it's the *ka-ching* of the screen door snapping shut again, the same rush of chilly air, the same scent of cologne, only now a bit faded, as the boys have left some of themselves in the house. We make sure each Elvis is facing the right direction. We wash out the ashy coffee mug and the sticky plastic tumblers. We take our places back in my bedroom, Dina and Bobbi Jo camped out in sleeping bags on the floor.

There are a lot of things we don't know. In a few weeks, we'll watch grainy video of a man named Rodney King beaten by police officers in California. In six months one of our cats will knock Hawaiian Elvis off the shelf, chipping a few flowers in his lei on the way down. My mother will gasp as his cork head pops off and bounces on the new carpet, bracing herself for a river of whiskey that never comes.

In a year, Dina and Bobbi Jo and I won't be friends. I don't know how to maintain friendships. They always wilt, then die like cut flowers, plants I don't know how to care for. In three years Keith will be a senior, and he'll host a drinking party at his house while his parents are away. There will be a boy named Curtis there, and he and Keith will have an argument no one will remember. Keith will kick Curtis out of the party, only to arrive at school the next day to learn that Curtis's car hit a tree and he died on the way home.

I'll see Keith slumped in the hallway outside the guidance counselor's office the next day, his head down, rib cage pulsing with staccato sobs. I'll hear a mandolin in my head. *Oh no, I said too much. I haven't said enough.*

★ ★ ★

Kids can be so cruel. Adults like to say this, as if teasing is some silly little rite of passage, but they don't know just how bad it can get.

Now that I'm in junior high, Samuel and I will never be in the same school together, and I've lost my shield, my blond-haired safety net, always there to catch me. My mother is suspicious of me, I know. She wants to know why Dina is my only friend, wants to know why no one else is calling the house for me. *When Linda was your age, the phone started ringing off the hook. Not just girls, but boys, too,* she says, reminding me of my failure, never letting me forget what I could be. My mother doesn't understand why it's so difficult.

"I practically dressed in rags," she says. "My family was the poorest on the street and I still made friends with the Gibson girls, the most popular girls in school. They were always trying to make me over—loaning me dresses and offering to set my hair, but I was happy to be their project. Why can't you be someone's project?" she wants to know.

I'm standing in the lunch line by myself. The cafeteria is a chamber of sound, voices bouncing off tables and chairs, hard ceilings and floors. Dina doesn't eat lunch, uses the time to paint her nails instead. There's a light-haired boy standing behind me. He's shorter than me. I don't know him, but I can feel him inching closer and closer to me until his breath is on my neck. "Hey, shit-ass," he says to me. I don't turn around. I pretend I can't hear him. "Shit-ass, I'm talking to you," he says, tapping me on the shoulder this time. Kids at the table next to the lunch line are paying attention now, laughing at me, at this boy whose name I don't know. "Look at her," he says to his audience. "She looks like she has shit in her ass."

I glance around the room for Heather Grain. I can't find her, but wonder if she's behind this, if she put the boy up to it. What does she offer boys to get her way? I think about leaving the lunch line, but I have to eat, and don't know where I would go anyway.

Most days, I feel like I'm falling down into a well, like baby Jessica. The difference is that no one wants to save me. Perhaps I am unsalvageable. If only I could come down with some disease, something life-threatening, then the kids at school would feel bad for treating me so poorly, and maybe at my funeral they would cry and cry uncontrollably and wish that they had done something to make me feel better, my casket covered with single roses and teddy bears and chocolates I can't eat because I'm dead, and my grave would become a shrine to all of the forgotten children, the ones without friends, without mothers who understand them.

# CHAPTER 18

# See a Penny, Pick It Up

The dreams haven't stopped, they've only become brighter, more vivid. I find myself running through empty caves, writing words on the walls that I cannot read. I find myself falling down six flights of stairs, landing on my bed with what feels like a bounce, yet my body doesn't move in real time. I dream of my own death, my funeral, magazine articles about me that will be published in *Good Housekeeping* to warn parents to pay attention to their children, so they don't end up like me.

I dream a lot about going to the bathroom, see myself slumped over the toilet, trying to dry myself between my legs, but the toilet paper comes back red every time. Sometimes I wake up with toilet paper wadded up in my underwear. I see myself trying to pee but crying instead, because I can't, but the feeling, the sensation to go is so strong it breaks me in two and I crawl back to my bed.

All of this happens like a movie I see in my head. I don't participate in my dreams, I observe them. I see myself as a character, a three-dimensional object I can move with my mind. I don't speak in dreams, no one does really. Communication takes place subliminally, or through feelings. I don't know how I know these things, but I believe there is something wrong with me for knowing them.

I dream about falling stars. I dream about an empty sky. I dream about walking alone in the middle of an empty road that looks like Washington Avenue, but I can't be sure. None of the landmarks are the same. I wake up hungry or thirsty, like I've been walking for miles. I wake up sweating or cold, sometimes holding on to my Alvin doll so tight I'm choking him. I spend mornings in the bathroom, wishing I could vomit, wanting to empty myself, but I'm too afraid to stick my finger down my throat. Maybe my toothbrush would work better. I have a sensitive gag reflex, it probably wouldn't take much. I try to eat a cotton ball because I think it must taste like a cloud. I wake up and feel like I've been drunk all night. I keep waking up every day, asking myself *Where have you been this time?* But no one answers, no one ever answers. I can't hear myself inside my head anymore. I'll walk into a room and feel a thousand feelings at once. They flash somewhere in the back of my brain, so quickly I can't count each one, but I know I've felt them and I know they stay with me. There is so much room inside me, yet I feel uncomfortably full.

I sit on my bed for hours after school, just thinking about existence, about how sad it all is. You are born, you live, and then you die. What happens in between? You might end up marrying a man who goes and shoots people in a factory. You might be the security guard working that day. You might get pistol-whipped. You might be the kid next door who becomes paralyzed one night and doctors poke a hole in your throat. You might be the little girl who falls into a well and sings into the echo of a long pipe until they pull you screaming and bloody into daylight, wrapped in gauze like a child mummy. Or you might be the one who must watch it all, who must store it away for no good goddamned reason.

As we age, my family gets bigger. Not in physical size, but in some other way. Somehow there is more space between us as we get older, the edges of our individual spheres expanding until we are miles apart, spinning separately. Occasionally, we wave to each other through the glass, smooth sheets of flint that have always been there, always determined our boundaries. I float along through adolescence, a missile, unguided, simply wandering through my orbit, hoping to collide with something, anything. Near the end of eighth grade, I find her.

Her name is Jessica Sienna, and although she is smart, she pretends not to be. She gets Ds in English, and blows off an entire week's worth of assignments in math, and she gets into fights in the crowded hallways—pulling a girl's hair as she passes, or whispering "Bitch" to someone under her breath. She writes on her jeans with permanent magic marker and pierces her own ears with needles. She even cuts her hair herself—an asymmetrical bob—shoulder length on one side, short and spiky on the other, stiff with Dep gel. She tells me how it feels to give a hand job, to punch someone in the face, to down a shot of vodka.

Suddenly, I'm following Jessica down the hall, conspiring with her at lunchtime to skip seventh-period math and sneak out to the gas station where she says the guy behind the counter will sell us Parliaments in a box, and we can lie in the woods behind East Park and smoke and drink pop and tell dirty stories.

Jessica's power is fluid, always moving, sticky and alive. I can feel her heat as we sneak out the side door of the junior high, run as fast as we can to that gas station, the sidewalk almost tripping us with its shifting cement plates. We learned about tectonics in science class, learned about continental drift. I'm sure that I'm a continent, too, that Jessica and I are simply doing what we're made to do—drift away from our families toward each other until we're so far out we might not remember how to find our way home.

I don't eat much, and I see myself getting skinnier and skinnier, my mother praising me with each pound lost, praising me when I push myself away from the dinner table after only a few bites of green beans. She wants me barely there. If I take up less space, there's more room for her—in the world and in our house, where she seldom speaks to my father. He's perpetually out hunting some sort of game—turkeys, rainbow trout, female deer. His jacket smells like blood and animal fur when he returns, his old yellow cooler parked on the kitchen rug, the cats sniffing around his boots for remains of flesh, for anything to taste. My mother cooks liver and onions, flank steak, breaded trout, my father's filet knife flexible and waiting on the swirled countertop, empty glass bottles of Coke drying in the sink.

Linda is perpetually facedown on her bed, her mouth pressed into the pillow, pink telephone receiver buried in her ear. I think of seashells, the earpieces they use in *Fahrenheit 451* to listen to sounds and music and advertisements, everyone plugged in to a constant stream of noise. Linda's boyfriend does most of the talking. She just lies there and hums into the mouthpiece, her lips coated with cotton candy lip balm, her toes wiggling at the end of the bed. Her boyfriend must sound like an ocean and she is getting lost in him. I want a boy to do that to me.

I imagine a boy's fingers rubbing me instead of my own. When I get in bed, I pretend the bedspread is a boy on top of me, his breath panting in my ear while he touches my center, the space that tunnels inside me. All I know is that it feels good to touch. I don't know why, but it does, and sometimes it's so intense, I have to bite my tongue as hard as I can to keep from calling out.

Jessica Sienna must be my good luck charm, because not long after we become inseparable, something amazing happens. A boy notices me. His name is John Wise and he is one year younger than me—tall and brown-skinned, sweet and outgoing. Jessica and I have stayed after school because we don't want to leave each other, don't want to go home. We're sprawled out in the hallway outside the gym, writing on each other's arms and chewing giant wads of bubblegum. We blow bubbles that grow bigger and bigger until they pop and smack our faces, then lick off the pink strings with our tongues.

Jessica says this will make boys think of sex, so I blow and lick as if my life depends on it. John Wise walks by in jeans and Air Jordans, eyeing us like sale items on a rack.

He is taller than me, which I like right away. And he is exotic—his light brown skin the color of a Tootsie Roll. There aren't many black kids in Connellsville, so he is the other, something different. He wears his hair in tight little curls cropped close, his face thin, his eyes deep and brown. He notices me right away, says something that I recognize as flirting. I've watched other kids flirt, having sex with their voices. I can get wet between my legs just listening, even though they aren't saying anything sexy. It's the way they say it, the soft tones, the laughter, the light touching of someone's shoulder, the anticipation of what could happen if everyone else in the room went away. Words dripping with something sticky like syrup. I think this is what Def Leppard is singing about, what Joe Elliott must imagine when he sings "Pour some sugar on me," the one-armed drummer beating the floor tom in the background.

John asks for my phone number and I give it to him, thinking he won't call, but when I get home later that evening, there is already a message on the fridge for me, John's name and number written in Linda's lopsided print. We talk for an hour that night and again the next night, our voices making matching sounds. I purr when I talk to him. My voice changes. It goes up an octave and every sentence is suddenly deliberate.

After a week of talking on the phone, John decides he wants to kiss me, so he devises a plan. We'll both ask for hall passes during second period, at 9:00 a.m., and we'll meet in the metal phone booth near the auditorium. There are only three classrooms in that hallway near the auditorium, which has been closed all year for asbestos removal. Yellow caution tape is wrapped like ribbon across the double doors, and for a moment I contemplate cutting my way inside, lying down on the cool of the tile floor near the stage, John's body grinding on mine in the dark. But no, I don't want to risk getting caught, and I'm not sure how dangerous asbestos is, although I know workers handle it daily at the factory, peel it from glass bottles with their bare hands.

John and I meet in the phone booth and we kiss, a long wet kiss with moving tongues that may or may not know what they are supposed to do. He puts his hands on my waist while he leans down on me and I feel tingles in my legs, my knees nearly buckling when I finally walk back to class.

When Jessica presses me for details later, I can't remember much—just John's lips moving toward me, closer than I've ever been to a boy's face. Did I close my eyes? I don't know. Did he have a hard-on? I don't think so, but how would I know? I know I wiped my mouth afterward and smiled. I know I couldn't seem to bring myself to talk, didn't want my voice to interfere with the electricity of the moment.

That evening on the phone, John decides he needs more of me, so he invites me to come to his house this weekend. He says that his parents won't be home on Saturday. They're leaving him and his little brother alone for the day while they go shopping in Pittsburgh. We decide I can walk to his house from mine, but I need an alibi, just in case my parents realize that I don't take walks.

It's settled—I'll say I'm walking to Dina's house, even though she and I aren't friends anymore. She's been catapulted into the stratosphere of popularity. As the high school boys started sniffing around her, they were disappointed that she kept bringing the ugly one with her everywhere, so I simply had to go. At first it was subtle—she'd forget to call me back or couldn't stay long when she came over. Then the distance started expanding, the tension warmer, warmer, then hot as coals. We could fill entire rooms with it.

One day, at her house, while Dina was in the bathroom, I snooped in her nightstand drawer and found a note from Tiffany Showalter, a petite beautiful cheerleader who was starting to hang out with us. The note seemed to be full of inside jokes, as if it were written in another language. Tiffany signed it "Y.B.F.I.T.W.W.W.," which everyone knows stands for *your best friend in the whole wide world*.

Finally the tension came to a head when we were all at Bobbi Jo's house—Dina, Bobbi Jo, Tiffany Showalter, and me. We were celebrating Bobbi Jo's church confirmation. Her family served finger foods and a cake with thick white icing. The four of us girls ate our cake on the front porch, the adults ate theirs inside. I ate one piece of cake, then went back inside for another. When I came back on to the porch, Dina and Tiffany were laughing uncontrollably, snorting and hiccupping and trying not to choke on the dainty bits of cake they were feeding themselves. I wanted to know what they were laughing about.

Dina said, in short breaths between laughs, "Don't worry about it. You had to be there." I felt a shaking start to build up inside me, a moving energy like bubbles in a pop bottle that sputter until they are finally released. My heart, my lungs, my hands, everything was warm and trembling. Tiffany kept laughing, but Dina stopped. Her face turned freezing cold and she gave me this look right in my eyes, a look that said *I don't love you anymore*.

I had to do something with the shaking inside, so I put my plate down on the porch swing, then dug into my slice of cake with my fingers. I dragged a wild and ragged scoop of sponge and sugar into my hand. I walked up to Dina and smeared it in her pretty face. Dina gasped the exaggerated gasp of a cartoon character, wiped the cream from her eyes and yelled at me.

"What the fuck is *wrong* with you?" she said. I didn't know how to answer her question that day. I still don't.

At first I worry that while I'm meeting up with John Wise my mother will call Dina's house looking for me, but then I remember my mother doesn't care where I go, doesn't even seem to notice that I've been bringing home mostly Cs and Ds on my report card this term, that I've been wearing short skirts and black stockings to school, caked-on foundation I've stolen from Linda's makeup bag, my bangs teased and sprayed into a peak over my head.

On Friday, I practice the route to John's house in my mind a hundred times, go over the plan with Jessica, try on outfit after outfit as she stretches across my pink bed, watching. "He won't care what you wear," she says. "You won't be wearing it for long."

My eyes start to water at her suggestion, and I work to hold in the tears. Is it possible to fear and desire something at the same time? I'm having cold feet. "What if it hurts?" I ask Jessica.

"Getting fingered by a boy doesn't hurt," Jessica says. "It feels the same as when you do it to yourself."

"But I've never done it to myself," I say. "I just rub it. I've never actually put my fingers in there."

Jessica's eyes get darker and wider, and she puts a fingertip up to her lips as if to silence me since Linda is just next door to us in her bedroom, probably facedown, listening to the waves of her boyfriend through the phone's round speaker holes. Jessica leans in toward me, her silver wire earrings dancing from her freckled earlobes. She pushes me down on the bed and unzips my jeans quietly. I stare at the ceiling, examining the swirled patterns of plaster and pink paint. Jessica takes my hand and slides it inside my underwear. "Now," she says. "Just find the hole and push."

# CHAPTER 19

# All the Day You'll Have Good Luck

It's Saturday, the day of my secret meeting with John Wise. I take a long shower. I read in *Seventeen* that you can rub a little lemon juice on your thighs if you're worried about your smell down there, but my mother only buys lemons in the summer to make her sweet lemonade.

Two o'clock comes and I call Jessica one last time and the plan is set in motion. I walk alone farther than I have ever walked alone. With no one to talk to, my mind runs through the dirty French movies I watched on Cinemax as a child. *Lady Chatterley's Lover, Emmanuelle.* I knew they were bad, but I watched them anyway, the sound turned down all the way so I couldn't hear the sounds they made, could only see bodies moving over and under other bodies, limbs and hair and flesh. I imagine the way John will pull my shirt off over my head, me raising my arms to make it easier for him. I imagine how it might feel when John presses himself against me, something hard inside his jeans. I imagine us under the sheets of his bed, our naked bodies underneath doing the things that I haven't seen yet. They don't show those parts in the movies.

When I knock on John's door, he answers in gray sweatpants and no shirt. His chest is hairless and lean, square outlines of muscle on his stomach. He pulls me in and shuts the door, kisses me hard. That's when I feel it for the first time—that hardness inside his pants pushing on me. It feels long and thin, but brutally hard, harder than bone. How is it even possible? It presses on the zipper of my jeans, and I let out a little sound, almost a cry, not quite a moan. John's little brother, who is ten years old, is watching cartoons in the living room, so we sneak into John's bedroom and lock the door.

"What if he knocks?" I ask.

"He won't." There's an authority in his voice that calms me. John starts to lift up my sweatshirt, so I raise my arms. It's all happening just like I want it to.

John reaches around my back, starts trying to unhook my bra. His hands are fast and clumsy, they're pulling and tugging at the clasp, the elastic stretching. "Here, I'll do it," I say.

I take off my bra and throw it on the floor but quickly cover my breasts with my hands. I back up until I'm against the wall, John sitting on his bed, which suddenly strikes me as a little boy's bed—sheets decorated with cars and trucks in primary colors. "Come on, I want to see them," John says, so I put my hands on my waist and let him look. He walks toward me, takes his hand and slides it down the front of my pants. I unzip my jeans to give him room, push them down, see them crumpled in accordion folds at my ankles.

I slide my underwear down, too, and as soon as I do, John's fingers are reaching for me, his fingers fumbling around until he finally pokes one through the center of me. I let out a little sound, just a small puff of air. It does hurt. John is poking around in me, one finger, then two, then three.

As quickly as he started, John pulls his fingers out and away from me, sits down on the bed. He motions for me to sit next to him and it occurs to me that we're barely speaking. Our bodies are doing all the talking. Anything we need to say can be said with arms and legs and fingers and eyes. John grabs my hand and pushes it down his pants to feel him. It's smooth and hard, and I hope I don't have to look at it, am suddenly terrified of what it might look like, this hard flesh in his underwear.

My eyes are closed so tight. I hope he's not looking at me. I keep moving my hand up and down on him, while he grunts softly and I imagine myself getting smaller and smaller, until I disappear completely in the folds of his little-boy bed.

★ ★ ★

On Monday, I write "I love John Wise" on all my book covers. In my family we use leftover brown grocery bags from Warehouse Groceries to cover textbooks. It's almost like wrapping a Christmas present, something my mother does to perfection, exquisite corners and neat folds. You don't have to use much Scotch tape if you know what you're doing. My book covers are usually bare, with only the name of the subject written in black magic marker. History, science, English, so boring and plain, just like I used to be, before Jessica, before John. But now I have a boyfriend, and I write his full name all over my books and notebooks, record my exclamations of love with big fat hearts and loopy cursive writing. I can walk down the halls clutching a math book in my folded arms, the message "Karen loves John Wise" staring at everyone as they pass.

Not only do I have a boyfriend (knock on wood), we went to third base. The first boy I ever kissed, the first boy who ever called me on the phone and I've already held him in my hands. I feel power bouncing off me as I walk down the hall.

"Does this make me a slut?" I ask Jessica at lunch. She just smiles.

"What do you think?" she says, and we both laugh.

By fourth-period history class, everyone knows about John and me. Amanda Craven walks up to me before the bell rings, before Mr.

Sleasak strides into the room and takes roll, his beady eyes shining like a toad's. He usually wears striped short sleeve dress shirts that are too tight, his belly distended painfully over his belt buckle. Amanda is concerned, speaks to me in hushed tones. We aren't exactly friends, but used to share a table in first grade, a bond that has linked us over the years, even though Amanda is one of the popular girls now. She lives up in the clouds with Dina and the others.

"John's telling everyone he fingered you," she says in a whisper. She is concerned—I see that in her eyes.

"It's okay," I say. "He's just telling the truth." I want her to know that it's not a rumor, that I really have done it, like I know she has—with Mike Schiffel, a ninth grader, under the bleachers at the first home football game this year.

She smiles an odd little smile. She thought differently of me, thought I was the strange little girl I used to be in elementary school. She doesn't know what's on the inside of me now. No one does.

I step off the school bus Monday afternoon and make my way down Isabella Road, red brick peeking out from holes in the asphalt. My dad says they paved the road right before I was born. I walk to our house, number 409. There is no number 407 on our street because ours is a double lot. There used to be two houses here, 407 and 409, two giant Victorians that nearly touched each other. I imagine they had turrets or cupolas, those little round castle-like domes with iron spires on top. Weathervanes, lightning rods, whatever they are, I'm sure the former houses on our lot had them.

The houses were old and eventually condemned in the 1960s. Domer Dale, a local land developer, bought the houses in 1970, had them torn down. Then he built our house in their place—a red brick ranch with a peaked roof and a sprawling yard, a driveway leading out into the gravel alley. My parents bought the house before it was finished, waited out their time in my mother's small second-floor apartment near the factory. When the house was complete, Dale asked my parents which house number they wanted, and they picked 409. *Sevens are bad luck,* my mother says.

*But I always thought sevens were good luck.*

*No, no, no,* she says, shaking her head. *Silly girl, that's how they try to trick you.*

I'm not home from school for long when the phone rings. I answer.

It's Tommy Ohler, John Wise's best friend. There is a commotion in the background, movement and a loud television and what sounds like Tommy's attempt to cover the receiver with his palm.

"John don't like you no more," Tommy says.

Silence on my end. I can't think of anything to say.

"Okay?" He sounds like he's getting mad. There is laughing in the background now, and cartoons playing at top volume.

"Okay." My voice is small, barely audible. *Click.* And just like that, he's gone.

# CHAPTER 20

# Something Old, Something New

The summer after eighth grade, I float from the swimming pool to the basement to my bedroom. In August, my sister Pam gets remarried. Her new husband is named Allen. He drives a red Nissan sports car. He's an insurance salesman, and his company is transferring him to St. Joseph, Michigan, a small town on the shores of Lake Michigan, one of the Great Lakes. I learned the acronym HOMES in school to remember all the names—Huron, Ontario, Michigan, Erie, Superior. I don't want Pam to leave Connellsville. Pam's the only person I've been spending any time with this summer.

Linda is about to be a senior, and rarely home, consumed with dating and parties most of the time. Linda barely speaks to me, and when she does, it's because she's getting ready to go out and she's ordering me to stay home and watch over our father while he cleans the pool. "You know he can't swim. You need to stay here and watch him," she commands. As if I have anywhere to go.

Pam comes over to do laundry and I'll make her laugh by pantomiming Queen's "Bohemian Rhapsody" or making Charmin do Stupid Pet Tricks like I've seen on *Late Night with David Letterman*.

And Pam's been taking me to the Fay-West Skating Rink with her friend Junie and Junie's two little kids—Gwendolyn and Stevie. We rent brown roller skates with bright orange wheels and eat really soggy pizza they serve at the concession stand. I've just learned how to skate backward, so that's all I want to do. The rink's owner, Rudy, a fiftyish man who wears all black and slicks his oily hair straight back, likes to announce each special skate over the loud speaker in his nasally monotone. "Couples skate," he drones into the microphone in his little DJ booth, pink fuzzy dice dangling above his head.

The walls of the rink are carpeted, the floors polished. During couples skate, Pam and I take to the rink together, skating to dreamy songs like "Take My Breath Away" and Pam lets me skate backward, steering us around the slick wooden circle while the colored disco lights strobe in darkness. We pass girls and boys skating awkwardly, their hands on each other's hips, around each other's necks. After the song is over, Rudy comes on the loud speaker again. "All Skate." The lights come up and all the non-couples pour back onto the rink. Junie and Gwendolyn and Stevie come racing toward us, and the five of us hold hands, make a living wall as we skate around and around.

Pam and Allen are moving in two weeks, and I want to go with them. Pam's daughter, my niece Samantha, isn't moving with them. She's staying in Connellsville to live with her father, who is newly sober and also newly remarried. Samantha is ten years old now—old enough to decide which parent she wants to live with. Pam is heartbroken that her daughter didn't choose her. I hear her crying to Junie in the kitchen one afternoon, while we're at Junie's house. I'm supposed to be entertaining Gwendolyn and Stevie upstairs, but I can hear Pam's sad voice wafting up through the vents in the kids' bedroom.

This could be a second chance for both of us—Pam needs a daughter and I need a mother. No one at school will miss me if I just don't show up on the first day. No one will even notice the empty desk in homeroom. No one will hear the silence after my name is called. After a few days, someone will report "I heard she moved to Michigan," and I will become a ghost, a legend, and John Wise will be left to wonder what would have happened if I'd stayed.

★ ★ ★

I exhaust my mother with all this talk of moving to Michigan. These are her words, not mine. My mother is easily exhausted by conversation, and the proof is in her eyes. They become dark and dull when I speak. They look straight ahead, never directly at me. She is perpetually in motion—it's difficult to make her stand still. She cleans the house every week, beginning with the basement and ending days later in her bedroom. As soon as she's finished, she starts the entire process over, because surely dust has already collected in the time it took her to work through the entire house.

She takes on extra projects, too—like painting the shutters, or removing the windows to wash them, or ironing all the curtains in one afternoon. All this work keeps her from dad and Linda and me. She floats around the house, more like a presence than an actual person, her scent of Youth Dew and Soft Scrub lingering in the hallway even after she's gone to her bedroom to "rest her eyes."

My mother sends my father to talk to me one evening. I'm in my bedroom, which is still painted pink, eating the last of a bag of potato chips and watching the movie *Die Hard* on HBO for what must be the fiftieth time. I've cut the foil bag open with a pair of scissors, so I can lick up all the crushed bits of greasy goodness.

"You have to stop all this nonsense about moving to Michigan. It's upsetting your mother," he says. His voice is flat and sounds rehearsed, which is what happens when mother has given him specific instructions on what to say. My father doesn't like confrontation with anyone, especially me or Linda, and especially now that we're older. Most days I get the feeling that he isn't quite sure what to do with us, like we're equipment he's been given to use, but without a manual. He likes instructions and procedures, would prefer if we were molds of glass emerging from a furnace instead of teenage girls.

I don't even look at my father. We both sit there in silence, the last words of his sentence suspended in the air between us, until neither of us seems to remember why we're here. My father leaves the room and I just keep watching the TV, Bruce Willis playing John McClane in his sweaty white undershirt, his bare feet cut and bloody from the broken glass he's walking through.

★ ★ ★

Pam and Allen pack up the little sports car, hitch a rented U-Haul trailer to the back, and drive down Washington Avenue on their way to St. Joseph. I want to run behind the car, tears streaming down my face, but there's no dirt to kick up on our smoothly paved road, and I'm afraid it won't have the same effect as it does in the movies. No one is looking out the rear window of the car to watch me anyway.

I stay in Connellsville to face ninth grade, alone. When you have no friends, returning to school in the fall is dangerous. I haven't spoken to anyone from school all summer. Right after eighth grade ended, Jessica Sienna's parents found a case of Iron City beer and a box of condoms in her bedroom. Her parents allowed her one phone call, like the police do when someone gets arrested, which she used to call me and tell me that she was being sent to live with her aunt in Ohio. Now no one is waiting for me to step off the school bus that first morning. No one is waiting to compare schedules with me in the hallway.

I have Mr. Morrell for homeroom. He's legally blind and wears eyeglasses as thick as the glass block windows in our garage. He teaches history and, thankfully, I've never had him for an actual class, but I've heard people tell stories of how difficult he is. He always has a student helper who assists him with attendance and such. This person must also monitor the room so that no students escape, because even though they say that when you lose one sense, the others heighten, Mr. Morrell is also partially deaf and the theory is that if you are quiet enough, you can sneak out of his classroom without him catching on.

I have a partial friend in a girl named Michelle Benz. We have four classes together and she doesn't seem to mind that I've invited myself to her lunch table. I sit quietly with Michelle and her friends as I nibble on bread and butter from the a la carte line. Sometimes I'll bring fake homework to do when I'm done nibbling. Sometimes I'll spend ten minutes in the bathroom just standing in a stall listening to the toilets flush while other girls spray their hair and smack their lips after re-applying lipstick. In junior high, girls don't actually go to the bathroom to use the toilets, which means I can remain in a stall for as long as I need to and no one will notice.

It turns out that getting fingered once does not make you popular, nor does it give you a "reputation." It doesn't even register. I pass John Wise in the hall and it's nothing, no spark of recognition, as if I'm water vapor, the clouds distilling me into thin air when I walk by.

The only bright spot of my day is first-period English with Mrs. Lewandowski. There, we work on our daily vocabulary, using small paperback books that are supposed to be college level, featuring words I love, like ephemeral and lugubrious. There, I read a play by William Shakespeare for the first time—*The Merchant of Venice*—and Mrs. Lewandowski makes us memorize Portia's "Quality of Mercy" speech. It's here, in this class, I begin to fall in love with a different boy named John. John Banks. I swear it's not my fault. In fact, I blame Axl Rose.

Axl Rose is the lead singer of Guns N' Roses, and Linda can't believe he's my current crush, having recently eclipsed both Corey

Haim and Patrick Swayze. "What do you see in that drowned rat?" Linda asks when she finds me in my bedroom ripping Axl's picture out of an issue of *Tiger Beat* and taping it to my closet door.

"You wouldn't understand," I say. I'm starting to like offbeat characters, like Steven Tyler from Aerosmith and Pauly Shore, the VJ on MTV. Axl is fascinating with his thin strawberry blond hair, his always bandana-ed forehead, his high-pitched, raspy scream. I've nearly worn out my cassette tape of Guns N' Roses *Use Your Illusion,* and John Banks knows this. So when I return from the pencil sharpener and find that he's written the words "November Rain" on my desk, I smile. He's knows it's my favorite Guns N' Roses song.

Mrs. Lewandowski is calling each student up to her desk so we can recite the mercy speech to her for a grade. Everyone is nervous, but I know the speech like I know the speckles on my bedroom ceiling, years of staring up there, imagining stars, imagining boyfriends. John Banks is a real live boy (like Pinocchio!) and although he has braces, and looks like the Campbell's Soup kid, and his head is too large for his body, and his cheeks are always rosy, I show mercy, as Portia has instructed.

*We do pray for mercy, and that same prayer doth teach us all to render the deeds of mercy.* I have been praying for mercy, that part is true. I've prayed for mercy for years. Mercy from boys who called me "gorilla" because I had thick dark hair on my arms, the teasing so bad that I've started shaving my arms with a razor every morning. Mercy from girls who whisper "Bulldog" to me as I pass them, because my lower jaw sticks out due to my under bite. I begged my parents for braces, but the dentist told my mother they wouldn't help. They'd have to break my jaw to correct it, wire my mouth shut for six weeks while it heals, but I've never broken a bone, knock on wood, so my mother won't allow it, thinks it must be back luck to break bones on purpose.

I've thrown myself on the mercy of the world. I've said, "Please love me." John Banks is the only one who answers. He answers even though he was one of the boys who teased me our entire eighth-grade year at lunch. I was stuck sitting with John and Timmy Miner and Jeremy Wisoloski that year.

Our school has three lunch periods, arranged by grade—seventh-grade lunch, eighth-grade lunch, ninth-grade lunch. In eighth grade, I had Algebra I during fifth period, the period in one's schedule that determines which lunch you're assigned. Because my Algebra I class had all ninth graders and just four of us eighth graders, we had to eat during ninth-grade lunch. So the four of us were our own little eighth-grade island, and I was the only girl at the table. I was stuck with John and Timmy and Jeremy the entire year.

Each day I stood in line and got Timmy's lunch for him, partly because I had a crush on him and partly because I'd quickly discovered that I couldn't eat in front of John Banks. He'd find something sexual to say about the way I consumed a taco, mashed potatoes, even something as harmless as a bowl of chili. He harassed me about anything inappropriate he could think of—his awful questions becoming routine.

"So is your pussy as hairy as your arms? You know you have a mustache, right? Hey, are you really a guy?" He'd snort first, then laugh so hard that he'd eventually stop making sound, his giant silent mouth stretched wide open, his face exaggerated like a cartoon character who screams and you see their uvula dangling. I'd just stare straight ahead and work on not making any facial expressions whatsoever. I'm good at that, actually, and I'm able to win staring contests rather easily because of it. People can be laughing all around me and trying to get me to break and I can just sit there, stone-faced. Expressionless.

I ace my mercy speech and John Banks struggles through his, messing up the part about mercy becoming the throned monarch better than his crown. I'm staring at my desk. Beneath the words "November Rain," John's written his phone number and "call me" with two exclamation points.

I can hear the song in my head now, and suddenly the lyrics are taking on a double meaning. First there's part of the verse—*When your fears subside and shadows still remain, I know that you can love me when there's no one left to blame.* I am afraid, always have been. Afraid of robbers and murderers and curses and aliens. Afraid of being alone. Then there's the refrain, the part in the music video when Slash climbs on top of the baby grand piano and the orchestra starts the buildup right before the guitar solo—*Don't ya think that you need somebody? Don't ya think that you need someone? Everybody needs somebody. You're not the only one.*

# PART THREE

*Girl years are longer than boy years, our lives stretched out like taffy, like the bubblegum we chew, always trying to make the biggest sound when the bubble goes pop, explodes onto our lips. We are pink on the outside—ribbons and dresses and jelly bracelets and barrettes, and pink on the inside—our tongues, the smooth insides of our cheeks, the smooth insides between our legs. We are seas of pink floating inside seas of pink. We kiss and scream and jump and play "Ring Around the Rosie" until we all fall down, hoping the boys will catch up, knowing that eventually they will. And they'll lay us down and peel off our clothes and tell us to close our eyes and open our mouths and shhhhh everything will be okay. That's what a girl year is like—string enough of them together and you have something that looks like a life. It looks like love or obsession or lust or maybe something completely different, something we're not able to name just yet. The boys run in larger circles around our smaller circles, waiting for the ones who break the chain, who let go of the hands of the girls on either side. And our families aren't much help, the temperature around them somehow cooler than ours. They live in refrigerators, in wallets and mailboxes, in factories and banks and the glow of the television set during the eleven o'clock news. How will we find our way? We stare at the sky, watching for falling stars, watching the people we love, the people we want to love us back, our arms open, ready to catch something, anything. Surely there is life up there. Surely someday it will fall like drops of cream poured from the Little Dipper into our cupped hands.*

# CHAPTER 21

# One for Sorrow

I'm always falling in love with someone else's mother. Once you start looking for mothers, they're everywhere. I look for mothers who are more like the one I imagine myself coming from, as if I might be reborn if I find the right woman to carry me. I dream up adoption fantasies, dream myself rummaging in the wicker chest in my parents' bedroom closet. Dream myself finding original paperwork embossed with golden seals, the name of my birth mother, a name that sounds light, names that begin with vowels, my mouth full of air when I say them. Her name is music rising in the sky. *Amelia. Elyse. Olivia.* I always wake up right before I find her.

Stories live on in my mind long after they've ended. My mind is a dream world. Sometimes it's hard to tell what's real. I can remember being very little, probably six or seven, but the time line is fuzzy, difficult to pinpoint. I remember thinking *I get along with my mother now* as if I had crossed a certain point, a threshold, with her. As if things were getting better, even though when I think of this flashpoint in time, I can't remember the worse times that came before. That is starting to scare me, because when I look back now, I see mostly bad times, just a feeling of tension, of doom.

It feels like I've been walking on a tightrope toward my mother all my life, holding a long white pole for balance. I start at one end of the rope, on a tiny platform. My mother stands on the other side. I'm trying to get to her, heel to toe, heel to toe, my feet in soft ballet slippers. I'm not sure I can get to her fast enough.

John Banks' mother is easy to love, so I love her. I think she even loves me back. Her name is Polly and she is young and beautiful—long silky hair, gracefully thin body.

John Banks and I started "going together" toward the end of ninth grade, on May 1, 1992, at 9:17 p.m. We were both fifteen years old. We were standing in my bedroom, me leaning against my first CD player, my small collection of CDs shining in their jewel cases from a shelf tacked to the pink wall. My parents have repainted our house dozens of times over the years, but never my room. It has remained pastel pink, the walls still the color of oozing Pepto-Bismol, or thick insulation that looks like cotton candy.

After John asked me the big question, I said yes, then glanced at the digital clock on the face of the CD player, so I could remember the time. Numbers are important to me. My favorites are three, six, nine, and eleven. I've taken up numerology, my notebooks filled with pages where I've added numbers over and over, checking my math eleven times. In numerology, you can turn anything into a single digit. Just keep adding and adding until there is only one number left. When you add it up, 5/1/1992 becomes 1, the same number my birth date turns into. The two days are linked, somehow: the day I was born, the day I was reborn through John. Aligned in magic, a numeric language.

The Banks family lives on a patch of land on John's grandfather's dairy farm in Bullskin Township, outside Connellsville city limits. When I get my driver's license, my father worries about me driving down State Route 982 by myself, makes me promise to call as soon as I arrive safely. John's father works for the Department of Transportation. He drives a steamroller over fresh patches of asphalt, wears an orange T-shirt with the sleeves cut off. He isn't home much. John's mother welcomes me into their home like a daughter, his sister Missy, three years younger than us, like the sister she doesn't have. John gets jealous when I sneak into Missy's room to talk about Stone Temple Pilots or look at her most recent paintings, abstract portraits of Scott Weiland, the reed-thin lead singer with a shock of wavy red hair.

My mother doesn't like John's family, but that's not saying much, as she doesn't like anyone these days, including my father. They live on separate floors of the house—my father ensconced in the cool of the basement, reading the newspaper and *Field & Stream* magazine. My mother moves from her bedroom to the dining room table and back, taking turns resting her eyes and paying bills, writing checks with the refillable silver pen. Linda is away at college in Pittsburgh. When she comes home on weekends, she sleeps most of the time, waking to stumble into the kitchen and eat something sugary, Hostess fruit pies, their thick crust painted with a hazy white glaze.

There is never a shortage of sweets in our house. I eat Betty Crocker cake frosting straight from the can, entire boxes of Little Debbie Nutty Bars in one sitting. When I start to gain weight, I begin a secret exercise regimen in my bedroom at night. One hundred and eleven leg lifts from a Denise Austin aerobics tape I remember watching at Pam's apartment years ago. One hundred and eleven sit-ups with my feet on the floor, then 111 sit-ups with the backs of my calves resting on my bed. John likes my new body, traces my hip bones that stick out when I lie down.

I remember to work different parts of each muscle, to burn the most calories. I have to do these exercises so I can continue my nightly eating binges. I'm too afraid to make myself vomit, although I've flirted with pushing the handle of my toothbrush past my molars, making myself gag a few times. I always chicken out.

I'm rarely home, but when I am, the silence has its own temperature, the air degrees cooler than at John's house. I have my own phone line in my bedroom now, an artery connecting me to John whenever I need him, which is pretty much all the time. He is my teenage husband, my protector, my best and only friend. I call him every morning before school, at 6:11 a.m. We don't talk long. It's more of a check-in, making sure we're both still alive, that we've made it through the night.

John makes me kiss him in the hallway at school between each class, gets mad when I try to get away with just a peck on the cheek. He wants French kisses, at least three swipes, he instructs, which is how he refers to the movement of his tongue inside my mouth. One day, Mr. Saltz, a history teacher, catches us making out like this against a locker. He whistles for us to stop—a loud high-pitched whistle from putting two fingers in his mouth. He was able to find out John's name, but not mine. John was called to the principal's office the next day after morning announcements. All the students in his homeroom let out the mandatory collective *oooooooooooh* that happens when a kid gets in trouble.

The principal tells John to kiss me outside of school, which John thinks means next to the buses at the end of the day, so now I'm required to let him have his three swipes while kids watch from the windows, cat calling until my face turns red. I climb the three steps leading into the bus feeling like John has branded me, picturing his handprints glowing bright on my waist, my breasts.

Polly isn't the first mother I've fallen in love with. I have a history of them, beginning with Amy Nickels's mom, Bubbles, back in elementary school and continuing with Dina's mom, Teresa, in junior high. Teresa smoked Marlboro Reds and worked gigantic jigsaw puzzles that covered their enormous table in the formal dining room, always something in her hand—a cigarette, a piece of sky.

But Polly is the one I've fallen hardest for, deeply wishing I was her daughter. I'd rather be John's sister than his Baby Lynn, anyway. My middle name is Lynn, so he's given me this nickname, as if I'm his child now. He feeds me and undresses me, swaddles me in blankets in his room, then dry humps me violently while I close my eyes.

★ ★ ★

My mother has become a cat person. It started a few years ago, when she took in a lazy orange stray with long hair, tufts of fur seeping between the pads of his paws, his tail a plume in the air. She named him Midas, and I used to pretend that he could turn me to gold with a single touch, like the folk tale. The cat just started hanging around our yard one day. He even jumped in the Blazer when my dad opened its brown and white door to get in to go to work. *Strange for a stray cat to do that,* my mother thought. *He must really want us to take him in for some reason.*

After Midas was in our home for a few days, that reason was discovered. The cat is the reincarnation of my grandfather, JR, my mother's dead father. Now everything the cat does is analyzed. The way he saunters around like he owns the place, his lumpy fatness, the way he torments my cat, Charmin. *Midas hits her like my father hit my mother,* my mother says, on her hands and knees scrubbing the bathtub with Comet and a washrag she throws in the trash afterward.

I've had Charmin since third grade. She came to me because of superstition, the ways most things do. We sat eating dinner in a fastfood restaurant next to Green Gate Mall in Greensburg, two towns over from Connellsville. My mother always preferred Green Gate to Laurel Mall, which is closer in distance, but has become somewhat of a ghost town now that Metzler's and Montgomery Ward have closed. I was eating a kid's meal, a plastic-wrapped burger, a sleeve of french fries, and my prize inside was a folded-up poster of a black and white kitten posing in a basket with balls of multicolored yarn. I'd been asking for a cat for years, but was always met with silence, so I didn't really think much of tossing out the request yet again, inspired by my superstitions and the poster, which I thought was a sign. This time, my parents exchanged a look and my father said, "Let's go back to the mall, to the pet store this time."

I chose Charmin because she was the only kitten there who wasn't black. She's gray with a little patch of white at her throat. Black cats are bad luck, so I couldn't choose any of the three dark kittens in the cage who were trying desperately to climb the metal slats. Instead, I chose the fuzzy gray one who sat in the corner of the pen pretending not to notice me. After I made my selection, the pet store worker retrieved Charmin from the cage and handed her to my father, who held her briefly before she was whisked into a cardboard box with two round holes in the top for breathing.

I carried the trembling box through the mall as my family followed me. I rattled off possible names for the kitten—Downy, Snuggle, and Charmin were the extent of my suggestions. I felt pressed to find a name for her quickly, to claim her before anyone changed their minds about me having her. In spite of years of writing lists of impossible names for imaginary children, I could only think of household products. Somewhere near the food court, it was official. This kitten would be named Charmin.

She'd have plenty of nicknames over the course of her life, the string of which began with Babs, the name of a character I remembered from a short story in our first-grade reading book. Her nicknames bloomed from there—Babs, Babsilina, Babby Babe, Babbit, Babbi-tee, Babbi-tee-tee. I never really thought about where the naming came from, I just knew that this cat was an ever-changing creature. When she would disappear around the house and I couldn't find her for hours, I believed she was traveling through time. I pictured her in ancient Egypt with the pyramids, flying with Amelia

Earhart, riding the trolley in San Francisco, the familiar ding of the trolley bell from the Rice-A-Roni commercial.

Charmin was our first cat, and Midas arrived years later. After that, my mother began actively looking for stray cats to take in. They are her new children. My mother has dreams about Midas talking to her, dreams in which he says to her *I'm hungry, Mama,* and she feeds him with a baby bottle. My mother believes that she can find the rest of her dead family living through animals in the neighborhood. She borrowed a trap from a neighbor to catch a wild black-haired pregnant cat, kept her in our garage for weeks, the creature wailing and hissing, trying to bite our hands when we replenished her food dish.

One day, as I was leaving the wild cat after refilling her water, I pushed the button for the automatic garage door opener by mistake. I'd meant to flick the light switch beside it, but instead the door rolled up with its noisy lumber and the pregnant cat bolted down the driveway, her swollen belly waving a kind of goodbye to me as she ran. My mother cried all night for that cat, which she believed might have been her mother, though she'd needed more time to be sure.

Midas goes for walks on a leash. My mother bought a green collar for him, a lightweight lead for her to hold. The cat prances around the backyard, as if on parade. My mother waits patiently as he moves slowly, decides to lay under the burning bush for a while, or rub himself against the pink azalea blossoms. The cat doesn't mind, in fact he likes it.

One evening Midas manages to catch a low-flying crow even though he is tethered to my mother. She doesn't really see it happen, just the aftermath. She looks away for a moment, and when she looks back, Midas has the black shiny bird between his paws. It makes my mother nervous, because there are many superstitions surrounding crows, like the fortune-telling verse that describes your luck based upon how many crows you see together at once. *One for sorrow, two for joy.* To make matters worse, a crow flying low over your house is an omen of sickness approaching. The next day, my mother bleaches the baseboards, opens all the windows, sprays everything in the house with lemon Pledge.

My mother started setting out small bowls of cat food around the backyard, hoping to attract her family. My father helped by creating a box out of plywood from the basement Ping-Pong table we didn't use anymore. He lined it with old rags and newspaper for warmth. Finally, one morning, I looked out on the porch and saw a dirty white cat step out of the box. I yelled for my mother, even though that was forbidden in this house. Linda and I were to seek her out personally if we needed her. She wasn't an animal to be summoned with calls and whistles, she'd told us when were too young to master snapping our fingers let alone whistling.

But now, yelling is okay if a cat is involved. This one is pregnant, too, and I name her Veronica, after the Elvis Costello song. *Is it all in that pretty little head of yours? What goes on in that place in the dark?*

About a month after we take her in, Veronica is pacing around my parents' bedroom, yowling. Honey Louise leans into her for a sniff, and Veronica, who I've nicknamed Vern, takes a swipe at the dog with one white paw. Honey Louise lets out a little yelp and backs away into her corner of the room, the old yellow and green afghan I used to masturbate under as a child spread out for her, a make-shift dog bed. All of our animals have middle names, thanks to me. Veronica's middle name is Ghost, because when we found her (or when *she found us* as my mother says) she was so dirty that her white fur looked oddly transparent, like an apparition of a cat instead of a real cat. Charmin's middle name is Tuesday. Not because we brought her home on a Tuesday, but rather after Prince Tuesday on *Mr. Roger's Neighborhood*, which is filmed at the PBS station in Pittsburgh.

Later that morning, Veronica Ghost makes herself comfortable under the corner dresser in Linda's room. Linda and I watch, our bellies pressed to the maroon carpet, as the cat opens herself, pushes out a total of six kittens—five white and one pitch-black. She eats the afterbirth, something we thought was an urban legend, but there it is, strings of dark red disappearing into Veronica's fanged mouth. The kittens are making newborn sounds, their mother rolling them around as she licks them into clean balls and they begin to root and nurse. I'm narrating the entire event, as if to record what's happening into an invisible tape recorder in the air. "Here comes another one!" I say to no one in particular.

My mother has purchased an old playpen from the classifieds in the *Daily Courier.* She has been preparing it for days, lining it with scraps of blankets and quilts. We will wait until Veronica has finished cleaning the kittens, then we'll transfer the family into the play pen, a safe container for them to live inside of for a while.

Sometime in the afternoon of their birthday, I'm sitting cross-legged on the floor next to the playpen, just watching Veronica and the kittens, their eyes still sealed shut, the way they root like little blind mice. I begin to notice that Veronica is nursing all of the kittens except one. One white kitten lies behind Veronica, its small body wedged between its mother's back and the netted wall of the playpen. The other five kittens suck and knead Veronica's wet stomach with their miniature paws, but this kitten is blocked from drinking. I watch the poor thing climb over Veronica, struggle to push its way toward the bright pink teats. Just when it looks as though it may start to eat, Veronica picks the kitten up by the scruff of its neck with her mouth, tosses it behind her back. As I watch, I feel something hard forming in my belly, in the very guts of me.

Something is not right. I think Veronica wishes to starve the kitten, but how could a mother do that to her child? The kitten cries and cries, sharp little sounds that pierce the air in the room, pierce holes in my body, holes through which my love for this kitten pours. My love forms a small lake of sadness around me, and I wade in it for just a few moments, until I finally stand and run for my father.

★ ★ ★

Dr. Meerhoff retrieves a small bottle of kitten milk from a small refrigerator. He takes a medicine dropper from his white coat pocket, fills it with milk, puts it to the kitten's lips. It's a girl, but I haven't named her. You mustn't name an animal until you're sure it will live. So in my mind she is "little girl" for now. Little girl sucks and licks desperately at the tip of the medicine dropper, and as she does, the milk bubbles from her nose. Dr. Meerhoff says she has a cleft palate, which means that there is a hole in the roof of her mouth through which milk gets re-routed instead of going into her belly. He says Veronica knew this, and that is why she was starving little girl. She didn't want to waste her milk on her.

"You can keep her alive, but you'll have to hand-feed her with a special dropper until she's old enough for surgery," Dr. Meerhoff says. "Or we can keep her for you and let her go." I think about those words together in the same sentence—*keep her, let her go*. I look at my father's face and I know that the kitten will always be little girl. She will have no other name.

We keep Veronica and the surviving kittens in the other room, which is a small room connected to our basement. We'll shut them in the other room so the dog and other cats won't bother them. On May 1, 1992, when I say yes to going with John, the kittens are only weeks old. After we make it official, John and I will go down to the other room, say we're visiting the kittens, but really he's pinning my stomach against the wall, rubbing the hardness of his jeans against my back while he holds my wrists, squeezes faint red rings into my skin. It begins this way and will always be this way, him shaping me into various poses, using me any way he wants.

# CHAPTER 22

# Two for Joy

At John's farm, we're in an old car that belonged to Nana, his dead great-grandmother. The car is from the 1950s, I think, pastel blue and white with fins, a metallic fish. It hasn't been driven for years, and sits in a peeling garage on the hill overlooking the Banks family trailer. It smells like mothballs inside the old garage, which is more of a shed, really. The car is covered in a heavy canvas, which we don't remove. We simply dive beneath the tarp, open the car door and shimmy into the back seat. It's dark inside the car, which is inside the canvas, which is inside the shed. So many layers to block out the sun.

John has condoms but gets frustrated trying to put one on, angrily throwing several into the front seat after realizing he doesn't know how to roll one onto himself properly. I see the slippery glint of a rubber crumpled on the dashboard like a banana peel as John decides it doesn't matter for the first time. He goes inside me dry and bare, covers my mouth with one hand when I tell him to stop. We are still fifteen years old. We are taking up all the oxygen inside the car.

Throughout that summer, John keeps getting what he wants. On a blanket within the cornfields on the farm. On my twin bed while my father is in the driveway washing the Blazer. We can hear the sound of the hose spraying water through the open windows. After dark, we tell my parents we're going night swimming, and we don't want to turn on the light inside the pool because it attracts June bugs and other beetles that buzz around on the surface of the deep end. John reaches down and slides the crotch of my bathing suit to one side, pushes himself in and out of me while I cling to him, my back brushing against the concrete wall of the pool. It's total darkness out here, only the stars when I look up at the sky instead of staring into John's eyes.

It's better in the dark like this. He can't see that I'm not looking at him, can't get angry when I look away. Darkness is better and being in water is better, cleaner, although I'll still go inside and scrub myself in the shower after John goes home, spit at my reflection in the bathroom mirror while I'm brushing my teeth.

I look over to the Ryan family's house for a moment and see the silhouette of Samuel sitting on their back deck, which is elevated enough so that you can look over our short fence and see the surface of our pool.

"My neighbor's watching," I whisper in John's ear. But he's not alarmed. He just stays inside until he's finished.

"Damn, that kid is weird," John says, as he pulls out and swims away.

# CHAPTER 23

# Three for a Girl, Four for a Boy

I have to make sure my radio is set to 93.7 FM before I turn it off. I have to arrange the pillows on my bed a certain way before I leave for school. I can tell if their placement is off, even by a few centimeters. My brain is a delicate instrument, able to detect the slightest change in surroundings. I have to call John every morning when my nightstand digital clock reads 6:11. I've never found out what happens if I don't. John thinks my superstitions are cute. He asks Polly to turn the car around after a black cat crosses the street in front of us. She drives a white Oldsmobile Delta 88.

John and I sit in the backseat together, a blanket stretched across our laps while we ride so he can finger me as much as he wants, which is often. He knows not to open umbrellas inside the house, knows I must pinch spilled salt from the table and throw it over my shoulder.

We have created our own cocoon—just the two of us. We write notes to each other during every period of the school day. I sign mine Baby Lynn. To our classmates, everything is sweetness and light, just like the Golden Age Miss Beers, my tenth-grade English teacher, talks about in class. We read the Shakespeare comedy *As You Like It*, learn to recite the monologue that begins "All the world's a stage and all the men and women merely players." If only that were true, then I could play the girl my mother loves. Shakespearean characters are often disguising themselves, men dressing up as women and vice versa, impersonations that are never questioned, always believable. The reader is the only one who knows.

Every piece of literature has a point of view, a way of seeing things. I like anything written in third-person omniscient, that god-like all-knowing narrator, who I picture sitting on top of a cloud, looking down at the characters, announcing not only their actions, but what they want, what they think, their dark dark desires. I look up *omni-* in the dictionary. It means "all; of all things," comes from the Latin *omnis,* which also means "all." That sound simples enough. I am concerned with etymology, word origins. I want to know where all things come from. We all have a creation story. Whether we're born or built in a factory, we all come from somewhere.

Boys and girls have always been different, but as we get older the differences become more sharply defined, the gaps between us wider, more ocean-like. There is a mystery, a code I want to crack, but I don't have the right numbers and letters, the right combination for the lock. I want to figure everyone out, want to figure out how other people make connections while I feel like I live on an island, *Lord of the Flies* except John is the only boy, and therefore, the only ruler. And I follow him. I jump over the moon for him, I jump over stars.

# CHAPTER 24

# Five for Silver,
# Six for Gold

While Linda's away at college, she and my mother get along, talk on the phone daily, my father worried about the long-distance phone bill as if my mother and sister are teenage girls, gossiping and giggling over the wires. But when Linda comes home to visit on weekends, or winter breaks, or those long stretches of summer months, she and my mother argue, Linda always getting in Mother's way no matter how hard she tries to lay low. My mother complains about washing all of Linda's dirty dishes, says Linda eats too many bowls of cereal, leaves too many spoons glued to the bottoms with sticky, half-dried milk. Linda washes the whole sink full of dishes one afternoon. I see her smiling to herself as she dries plates with a mauve dishtowel, happy to please my mother, to surprise her.

When my mother returns from work, she opens the silverware drawer, sees the dinner forks mingling with salad forks in the same compartment, fat soupspoons on top of the more delicate teaspoons, when it should be the other way around. My mother pulls the drawer clean out, dumps its entire contents on the kitchen counter. "If I want something done right, I'll do it myself!" she screams, and Linda goes back to the couch, covers herself with her dorm room comforter, Honey Louise curled at her feet.

Pam and Allen live in Florida now, Allen having been transferred from Michigan by the insurance company he works for. My mother is glad that we have family in an exotic location now, sees Florida as a humid dream-like place, a playground for Rich People and Beautiful People. During my high school years, we take at least two trips a year to visit them. My father drives us in the new Lincoln Town Car, a long silver car from the prestigious "Cartier Series," a step up from both the lower versions: the "Executive Series" and "Signature Series" that you see other people driving. My mother is proud to be the only person in town with a Cartier, even though it's still a used car. The official color is "pearl" according to Ted Dugger, the man who owns the Lincoln Dealership in Connellsville.

My mother has bought and traded in four Lincolns with Dugger over the years. She started with a white two-door Continental, then moved on to a red two-door Continental, then a burgundy Town Car that was better for us kids getting in and out, too much climbing into the backseat with a two door. Now, this pearl Town Car, the latest in her Lincoln history. Through the years, my mother has my father take a picture of her posing with each car.

My mother fixes her hair just so, teased throughout the '70s and '80s, permed now in the '90s. She wears something expensive looking, not something she'd wear to work. Her fake smile intensified in the photos, as if the camera is able to capture her mania in a way that can't be seen by the naked eye.

My mother is breaking, not just on the inside, as it used to be, but on the outside as well. I've been watching it happen since Linda went to college. My mother's body is deconstructing itself, showing signs of wear and tear from the repetitive motion of pulling baby food jars off the line, four at a time, her fingers poking their mouths like eyes. Her shoulders and neck give her trouble. She says she has bone spurs, like her father had, and I imagine the small metal star-like wheels that cowboys wear on their boots. I picture them beneath the skin around her collarbone, the soft flesh of her shoulders. Spur is a very old word, derived from Anglo-Saxon *spura, spora,* related to *spornan, spurnan,* meaning to kick, spurn. It was first recorded in English circa 1390, and means the generalized sense of "anything that urges on, stimulus."

My mother talks a lot about Sonny's wife, who still works at the factory where her husband killed four people, then killed himself right in front of her. The year I'll graduate from high school, 1995, will be the tenth anniversary of the shooting, and my mother knows this, is building and building for the eventual observance. Sonny shot himself right there in front of Shop 22. The noise from the factory floor was so loud, some workers didn't know what was happening until it was too late.

"Isn't there some emergency shutoff switch for the furnaces?" I'd wanted to know. "A way to stop all that glass if you need to?"

My mother replied, "Emergency? At Anchor, turning off a furnace is the emergency. Heaven forbid we stop making glass." She shook her head, disgusted with this place she's given so many years of her life to. "They're taking our bodies," she said when co-workers began dying from cancer.

We have to drive past Brooks Funeral Home on our way home from anywhere. It's just three blocks from our house. They have a small black display for words behind glass where Mr. Brooks posts the names of the people (The names of the bodies? Are they still considered people now?) who will be there for viewing. Every once in a while, we see Mr. Brooks standing at the open glass door of the display, a window that opens to nothing, to blackness, removing the small white letters, replacing them with new ones. If my mother is driving, she makes me look over and read off the names. She always knows someone, either from her childhood in South Connellsville, or the factory.

"Maybe it was all the asbestos," my father says, "or the clear glaze we used to brush on the bottles. When it got in the air, it made a lot of us cough." My father's throat is always sore, a canister on the counter full of Chloraseptic lozenges he eats like candy.

When I'm eighteen, away at college in Pittsburgh, getting served underage at one of the bars where the bouncers only ask to see your university ID, not your driver's license, I'll always order Rolling Rock in a bottle, look at the numbers stamped around the bottom— plant number and shop number and mold number, the tiny Anchor symbol, like an actual ship's anchor. I know all the codes on glass, my parents having taught me how to read them over the years. I'm a walking decoder ring, an interesting little bar trick, so I'll show my friends, anyone who happens to be drinking with me.

I'll get drunk, give the handsome bartender a $10 tip for every beer he places in front of me, tell him how these bottles were made by my parents, that they painted the designs on, too, green glass running through machines that stamp on the blue and white design. I'll tell him that my mother used to bring rare glass defects home for us, and my favorite was something called a bird swing. It happens when a thin strand of glass appears inside the bottle, stretched side to side, as if a miniature bird really could perch there, could really live inside the glass. I'll ask the bartender, "How can something so beautiful be a mistake?" but he won't answer. He'll only smile.

I'll tell him that once my mother brought home a Rolling Rock bottle with a mosquito trapped inside the paint, white splat of small insect body and spidery legs. I'll describe how I put the flawed bottle on the dresser in my bedroom, how I traced the fossilized bug with my fingers, my hand slowly inching itself across the bruised surface of the bar, toward his.

★ ★ ★

As I move through high school, my mother moves through anxiety, a small boat without an anchor floating through a tunnel that narrows, her claustrophobia flaring up more and more. As soon as I start my senior year, in the fall of 1994, she starts telling me how much she'll miss me when I leave the house. My father says it's just empty nest syndrome talking, that she'll be fine.

My mother is fifty-three years old now. She's been raising daughters since she was twenty, when Pam was born. That seems like a long time to have children around, a child body always nearby, always in a state of need. My mother takes sick leave from work a dozen times throughout the school year. She has stomach trouble, indigestion, aches and pains that wake her at night. She wakes my father, who wakes me, tells me he's taking her to the emergency room in Greensburg, forty minutes away. We have a small hospital right in town, but my mother doesn't want them knowing her business.

She doesn't mind missing days at the factory, the decrease in pay, tells me it's worth it just to be with me. She is focusing on me, like an intense camera or pair of high-powered binoculars. I can feel her concentration on me, warm rays that sometimes catch fire. She is jealous of John, jealous of the few girlfriends I have from marching band, where I'm a member of the color guard. We wear military-inspired uniform jackets, short white shorts over dark tan pantyhose, and white boots with tassels. We twirl flags and mark time with our feet. We make formations on the football field at halftime, learn the ten-yard lines, the one-yard hash marks. The moves we learn are called carves and push spins, windmills and presents.

My mother sits in the living room, pretending to read a magazine when I get ready to go to the mall with my friends on weekends. *You keep leaving me,* she tells me. *Why won't you stay?*

I don't worry about my mother's health. There doesn't seem to be anything wrong with her, no evidence of illness to support her symptoms. I look up psychosomatic in the dictionary. It's an adjective and it has two meanings: *1. (of a physical illness or other condition) caused or aggravated by a mental factor such as internal conflict or stress 2. of or relating to the interaction between body and mind.* Psycho- comes from the Greek *psukh,* which is *breath, soul, mind.* Soma from the Greek meaning *body.*

I can break words down, label the parts, the roots, the way we used to diagram sentences in Mrs. Swan's class. I loved the look of each diagram, the lines like tree limbs, little graphs like snowflakes. No two sentences looked alike. Sentences can be broken into words, words into roots, roots into letters. All that tree imagery calms me. I've grown up around trees, every sidewalk I walk scattered with fallen leaves or nuts, buckeyes, those big green seedpods kids call Monkey balls. So many things return to sex, return to our bodies.

★ ★ ★

It's strange with just the three of us inside the house—me, my mother, and my father, and the animals of course. We have five cats now and Honey Louise. There's Charmin and Midas, my reincarnated grandparents. There's Veronica Ghost and the one kitten we had to keep because we couldn't find her a home. Actually, we did find her a home with a childhood friend of Pam's named Judy. Judy's daughter had named the cat Ariel, after the Little Mermaid, but the little girl kept getting scratched, was too young for a pet, so the kitten was returned to us. She is all white, just like her mother, and I named her Sybil Elaine, taking her first name from the famous psychiatric patient with multiple personalities.

Elaine is one of my fantasy birth-mother names, an imaginary woman who might have given me up for adoption in another life. We also have a brown tabby cat, another stray my mother took in. She has white paws and a white mouth, but the rest of her is patterned like a bobcat, a wild animal. I'd wanted to name this cat Capote Lee, after Truman Capote and Harper Lee, the two famous writers who were childhood friends. I thought I might call her Cappi for short, but my mother stepped in before I could, started calling her Pooter. I refuse to acknowledge the name, ignoring the cat most of the time, just saying "here kitty" if I need to call her to me.

In Connellsville, the beginning of the school year means football games, and John is a starter on defense this year. I don't know what position he plays, only know to watch the field for his number, 95, which is lucky because it's also our graduation year. It must be a sign.

John and I have celebrated two anniversaries so far, each one with dinner at the Olive Garden near the mall in Greensburg. I saved the silver foil-wrapped chocolate mints our server brought us at the end of each meal. I'm storing them in the freezer so they will be safe, preserved. By now, our classmates see us as an old married couple. Two years and four months feels more like twenty-five when you're seventeen years old, and in love, which we believe we are.

We've pretended to break up many times over these two years and four months, many screaming matches, many phone conversations with tear-choked voices, but the cracks and divides were always filled in with my fear of being alone, my dependence on John to sustain me. I don't know who I'll be if I'm not his. Lately, we have something else keeping us together, something to bind us, an exciting new focus. Polly is pregnant.

It wasn't planned, John and I knew that before the announcement was made, John and Missy and me lined up on the couch in the tiny trailer living room, listening to Polly explain the news through tears. John is seventeen and Missy is fourteen and few parents plan to bring a new baby into that equation. Over the summer, I enjoyed watching Polly's stomach grow. She'd place my hands on her belly, let me feel the baby kicking inside.

On the Fourth of July, we sat together behind the trailer on green and yellow lawn chairs, facing the cornfields to watch fireworks being set off from the VFW down the road. It was just the two of us and the sky looked bigger than usual, we could see more open space, breathe a little more air, be a little closer to the natural world, to each other. Each boom from the fireworks made the baby inside Polly flutter and squirm, and she let out a little *Ohhhh* each time, then smiled and rubbed her stomach the way I always imagined a mother would.

The little girl is born after a football game, on a Friday night in October. *Friday's child is loving and giving.* And this baby has given us something. She's our fascinating little doll, John and I playing house with her, posing for pictures with her that come out looking like we're the parents, cradling the baby and each other and smiling the way new parents do. Polly names the baby Katherine and we all call her Katie for short.

Polly lectures us about safe sex and pregnancy. "Your dad and I were *careful,* too" she keeps telling us, but she never defines *careful.* Had they used a condom and it failed? Had John's dad pulled out? It's creepy to think about him, round and sweaty, his skin leathery from years of working on roads in the sun, on top of Polly, so light and pretty, but I think about it anyway. John decides that the condom must have torn, so we start using two even though he says it takes him longer to finish that way. It doesn't matter to me, I just make myself still while he does what he needs to do. There is no finishing for me. I'm starting to think there never will be.

I know so many of John's family's secrets, more than my own. I have seen them at their best and worst moments, because they've let me into their lives even when it's ugly and messy, even when it needs to be cleaned up. I get to see all of it. My family is sanitized, sterile. There are no messes in our home. If there are, we don't talk about them. Both sets of John's grandparents treat me like a granddaughter, getting me gifts for holidays, my birthdays. I am invited to everything, it's automatic. Wherever the family is, it's assumed I will be there, too.

One night, John's father comes home drunk, something that rarely happens. I've seen him drink a beer from the fridge here and there, at Christmas gatherings at Pap Hardy's, Fourth of July corn roasts, those kinds of things. But he's staggering drunk tonight, bursts open the door to John's tiny bedroom—it's really the laundry room of the trailer, only enough room for a twin bed and one tiny nightstand perpetually scattered with half-used deodorant sticks and Slim Jim wrappers.

John and I had just been talking, there's nothing to see. I think his dad was hoping for a show, like the time he opened the door to remind John about feeding the dogs and found me pinned to the bed chest down, while John dry humped me from behind. John and his friends call it "dry-racking," which sounds even worse, I think, but it's a safe staple of sexual activity for John and his circle of friends. They have to call it something unique, must have their own system of naming, their own way of talking about it.

John's dad starts tickling his toes, taunting him. *Come on, big boy, let's wrestle.* John doesn't want to, yells for Polly to get his dad out of here. Polly is a red silk scarf waved in front of a bull. John's dad charges at her and we hear her footsteps as she runs to the dining room. We run out of the bedroom, me following John along the carpet that is so worn in certain places it's been patched with silver duct tape. John's dad is doing one of those bits where when Polly moves right, he moves left and so on, as if Polly is looking in a mirror with a five-second delay and a distorted reflection, some strange monster version of herself.

John gets his dad's attention, distracts him so Polly can retreat to the living room with me and Missy, who is on the rocking chair holding Katie. Katie is happy, doesn't know she should be anything else. Missy and I give each other glances like sisters who grew up in the same house, soldiers fighting in the same war. We are four women of different ages and sizes, sitting in the living room of this old trailer, letting the men settle things.

*Come on, boy,* John's dad says, slurring all three words together like his mouth is a blender.

*It's the whiskey,* Polly tells me, as if it's just a matter of fact. *It's devil water.* She tries to make some nervous small talk, but I hear a thud over her tiny voice, then a crash of glass. We run into the dining room to find the table overturned, John's father underneath it, held in a headlock by John, whose cheeks are redder than usual, his forehead beaded with sweat. The crash was the sound of an antique glass basket falling to the floor. The basket had belonged to Polly's grandmother. Polly displayed it as a centerpiece. It was shaped like a country basket that would hold fresh eggs from a farm. It looked light and delicate but was actually quite heavy.

It's on the floor now, the glass handle split clear from the base. Missy hands Katie over to me and starts helping her mother scour the carpet for shards and slivers. It looks like it's been a clean break, but we can't be sure. I hoist the baby on my hip and she plays with my earrings, gold hoops John gave me for Christmas one year.

John's dad calls us a bunch of stick-in-the-muds, bounds down the hallway, and slams the bedroom door. He'll sleep it off. I walk over to John, Katie reaching her chubby little hands toward him. She smiles, laughs at his wide eyes as he picks himself up off the floor. Polly is still running her hands all over the carpet, cursing the devil and his water.

# CHAPTER 25

# Seven for a Secret
# Never to Be Told

John and I talk about getting engaged after high school graduation, that way we won't cheat on each other while we're away at different colleges. We talk about getting married right after we receive our degrees—mine in English literature, his in electrical engineering. But John says he wants to return to the farm after college, wants us to live there in his Nana's old place, the white clapboard house on the hill next to the shed with the silver-finned car we still use for sex. I want to live far away from Connellsville some day, in a big place like New York City. John wants to always live in the country, the way he was brought up, says it's not living if you can't walk outside in your underwear in the morning and take a piss from your porch.

I want to apply to colleges in big places, too. Colleges like NYU and Boston University and UCLA, but my mother doesn't want me going that far. She imagines a tether between us, a leash that will only stretch a certain number of miles. John wants me to stay home and attend the community college with him, the only place his parents can afford. Still, I request catalogs from these far-off schools, thick envelopes that arrive in the mail addressed to me. I shut myself in my bedroom and flip through their booklets and brochures the way I used to scour the Sears toy catalog at Christmastime as a child.

In spite of all this dreaming, I only apply to one university—the school in Pittsburgh where Linda is earning her degree in nursing. Luckily, I'm accepted, as I have no backup plan. I already know the campus, having helped schlep Linda's stuff in a rolling canvas cart up and down an elevator every summer and fall for the last three years. My junior high friend Dina has already been accepted to this school, so I'll know at least one person there. We stopped being friends after eighth grade, but that won't matter as much at college. In high school, she's a cheerleader with a beautiful body—thin legs, large breasts, everything teenage boys like. And she has long, flowing chestnut hair.

She'll be on Homecoming Court our senior year, will be one of the gorgeous popular girls walking down the aisle of the football field during halftime, the aisle that me and the other marching band members made for them, our flags and instruments held at an angle, a kind of salute to high school royalty. The points of the pretty girls' high heels will sink into the grass a bit near the fifty-yard line, and they'll wobble, but still look beautiful in their fancy skirts and suit jackets, life-size Barbie dolls, the executive version—Barbie in her power suit, her slim briefcase.

Leaving town after high school is the only thing I want right now, and although my mother seems to have been grooming me for it all these years, she's suddenly backing out now. She wants me to stay, says she's happiest when I'm around.

She used to have days of energy bursting like blinding white stars in between her dark bouts of sadness, but lately it's all sadness all the time. It's just her stretched across her bed, crying, rubbing her shoulders, crying, looking for pictures of her parents she hasn't seen in years, crying. Looking for her brother's hat from the Navy, tearing through boxes she's pulled from the attic, then remembering with a gasp that he was buried with it.

It's the morning of my high school graduation, and I'm rummaging around in the wicker chest in my parents' room. I'm looking for my School Days book, this little scrapbook my mother started for me in kindergarten. It has a page for every grade K–12, an empty square in which to paste that year's school picture. It has a pocket to store report cards and awards. I've been updating it myself since junior high, when my mother lost interest in the business of my growing up. I want to find it now so it will be ready to fill with graduation things, that fake rolled-up diploma they'll give me at commencement, my white hat tassel, a dried petal from the roses John will give me later tonight after sex in his mint-green El Camino. He'll pull them from under the driver's seat with a flourish, lay them on my naked stomach, a surprise in bloom.

In the wicker chest, I dig through old newspapers and hundreds of rolls of developed pictures still in their original paper packets from the photo department at Burns Drug Store. My mother now keeps her father's high school ring in a small velvet bag, and I take it out to inspect it like I always have, as if his engraved initials might have changed, as if the gold may have melted over the years. There are my father's Army papers, his discharge certificate. There are some drawings Linda did in kindergarten, stick figures and ink blots her teacher laminated for safekeeping.

Under all this, I see a plain manila file folder, a label on the tab with my name on it, last name first, first name last. I open it up and it takes me a long time to realize it's a medical file, my eyes scanning the black and white inside the folder, my eyes needing time to adjust as if the lights have just gone out in the room. It's a written report from a pediatrician, but the doctor's name is not one I recognize, not our regular pediatrician, the one Linda and I went to for years for shots and sore throats.

Inside the folder rest two sheets of paper. A form with my name and various vital signs—weight, height, temperature. And then an unlined page of observation notes, where the doctor has written in scribbled cursive *labia red, hymen torn, blood on pants.* So few words, yet they take up the entire page, each phrase scrawled on its own line, like a poem. The file is dated 1980. I was four years old.

Only a few moments have passed, but each one is unending, exploded into units that feel more like hours, like days. I float above myself and peer down at the girl at the center of the room, the girl who looks like she's just discovered something dead in the wicker chest . . . a severed foot, a shrunken head. I replay the scene over and over, watch the girl (for she is still just a girl after all) read the doctor's looping words, then close the file quickly and bury it away again, under glossy wet stacks of birthday parties and Christmases. She's so desperate to make it disappear, to send it back to where it came from.

## CHAPTER 26

# Eight for a Wish

I've done things I try to forget, and, sometimes, my mind succeeds in forgetting. It's my body that is stubborn, my body that keeps remembering. Sometimes my mind and body compare memories and they don't always match up. Psychosomatic, the second definition this time, *the interaction between body and mind.* How can they be so separate, while in the same person? I want to know where they intersect.

My body remembers playing what I called "the naked game" with my niece Samantha, Pam's daughter who is four years younger than me. My body tells me we were downstairs, in the other room. My body tells me I took my clothes off, encouraged her to do the same. That I started pretending the bare walls of the room were actually men who wanted to kiss and touch us. I walked up to the wall, pressed my naked body against it, actually began kissing the wall with my open mouth.

I don't remember what Samantha did. My mind remembers that she just watched, that she kept her clothes on. That I didn't touch her. That I only touched the imaginary men along the wood-paneled walls. I'm afraid to ask my body what it remembers.

My body remembers me saying to my mother, *I want to be a child molester when I grow up*, but that can't be right, can it? I try to re-create the scene in my mind. It's me sitting on the dining room floor in front of the sliding-glass door. I have an image of the sun shining in, a feeling that it is autumn outside, crisp leaves floating from trees. I have an image of my mother laughing at me in return. I have an image of an open box of crayons next to me, a coloring book on my lap. My mother is an artist when it comes to coloring with crayons. She makes the tiniest circles so that her pictures look soft, textured.

My body remembers kissing a man on the lips and him moving my head from side to side, his hands pressing on my cheekbones. My body remembers him saying *this is how big people kiss* and someone in the room laughing, an invisible audience. But my body doesn't remember who was there.

My body remembers asking Pam about our uncle Roger, the only living member of our mother's original family. I wanted to know what he was like, because our mother had stopped talking to him sometime after their father died in 1980. Pam said one time my mother took her to visit the family at the peeling yellow house on Atlas Avenue. Pam was about five years old. Our mother had put her in a dress, something girly, and she'd put tights on Pam with no underwear underneath. Something about panties under tights not letting your girl parts breathe properly. This is the way my mother still does it, which embarrasses me whenever I walk in her bedroom in the rare occasion of her putting on pantyhose, her thick triangle of pubic hair exposed, spilling toward her belly button.

Pam remembers Uncle Roger sitting in a chair in the living room. He told Pam to come over and give him a kiss. She stood at the side of the chair while he remained seated, putting his arm around her little shoulders as she gave him a peck on the cheek. Then he moved his hand down her back, lifted up her dress, slipped his hand inside her tights. He put one of his fingers between her butt cheeks, rubbed it back and forth slowly while the rest of the family chatted. The chair he was sitting in was against the living room wall, so no one could see what was going on behind Pam. She never told anyone, until I'd asked about him.

Now I'm holding this medical file in my hands and I'm remembering that night in my bedroom. How my mother caught me rubbing myself, blood on my underwear when I looked down. Was there blood on the sheets, too? When my mother worked night shift and my father and Linda were downstairs watching TV, I'd come upstairs, saying I needed to use the bathroom. I would lock the bathroom door—the only room in our house with a door that locks. All of our bedroom doors have smooth knobs without locks or keyholes.

Inside the blue-tiled bathroom, I'd take off all my clothes and touch myself all over while watching myself in the mirror. I'd pose myself in positions I realize now as sex positions. I'd stick my finger in my mouth, bite down on it. I'd try to suck on my own breasts, but they were too small and I couldn't reach them no matter how much I stretched myself, no matter how much I longed for them. I'd kiss my own arms and legs instead, licking all the salt off my skin. I'd get on my knees, press my left hand into my center, rub and rub until I reached the dew point. Standing up on rubbery legs, I'd wash my hands, flush the toilet so my father could hear the water running through the pipes, would think I was just going to the bathroom like a normal little girl.

Then this, another memory of the body. I'm not even in kindergarten, that feeling of not being old enough for school yet. I wake up in my parents' bed. I wake up crying so violently I make myself throw up. I have an image of my little body, wearing only a pair of pale yellow underwear, my long hair tied back in a ponytail. I have an image of me throwing up in the sink, over and over. Someone is using the toilet so I can't vomit in there like I'm supposed to. Where is Linda in this memory? I don't know. This is what I do know: I keep vomiting. I'm not ill; it's not the flu. I'm making myself throw up. I'm making myself get rid of as much of my insides as I can. Whatever has been in my body, I just want it out.

I've always known the word incest. I've looked it up many times over the years, each time hoping that the definition would change, that it would become something normal. When television shows would address the subject of child abuse, sexual or physical, I became excited, wet between my legs. I wanted to see the child get beaten or touched inappropriately. I wanted to see them suffer. Right before my eleventh birthday, a little girl name Lisa Steinberg was killed by her adoptive father in New York City, and the media attention seemed to open invisible floodgates of child abuse.

I remember our class being shown a video in school that year about a little boy who is invited to his neighbor's house to help fix a broken window screen. The neighbor, a fiftyish man with graying hair and a polo shirt offers lemonade and a few dollars as compensation. But when the little boy gets there, the man tells him to take off his shirt, says he must be getting sweaty from all the work. Then the man starts rubbing the little boy's back, tracing his shoulder blades with his fingers. The little boy does the right thing. He runs home to tell his mother.

I remember wishing the video was a "choose your own adventure" book instead, a book that lets you make choices for the main character. *If the little boy runs home to his mother, turn to page twenty-three. If the little boy stays with the man, turn to page thirty-five.* I would turn to page thirty-five and see what the man does to the boy. I would cover my eyes with my hands at first, watch the scene through spread fingers, but eventually my hands would fall to my lap, slide between my legs.

When I have sex with John, it never feels good and that doesn't make sense to me at first, but over time I realize why—I want to be the one in control, the one who can make someone pleasure me against their will. I want to be the vessel, the bottle, not the liquid poured inside, not the thing to be contained.

# CHAPTER 27

# Nine for a Kiss

I don't care about empty nest syndrome and how much more my mother might break without me here to hold the various pieces of her together. I'm going to college in Pittsburgh. I'm about to be away from my mother for the first time. I'm tired of being human glue. Birth order, I'll learn later, has a lot to do with this. I'm the baby, the peacemaker. I think the family won't exist without me. If I turn away, they will disappear because I won't be there to look at them. I have always been the observer, the cataloger, the reference librarian of our lives, my mind full of metal file drawers I can pull information from whenever I want.

John isn't happy with my leaving, either. He is going to the local community college and staying in the trailer with his parents and Missy and baby Katie, who is almost a year old now. He is going to call me every day, write me every day. He is going to come visit me so we can have sex in my dorm room. He has planned all of these things without me. He doesn't realize I want to get away from him, too, be free of him, too.

I live on campus, in a freshman dorm with no air-conditioning. Linda lives in a high-rise apartment on Mt. Washington, overlooking

Pittsburgh's "golden triangle," that city wedge in panoramic view during the opening credits of the local news, the fountain at Point State Park, the three rivers coming together, the bridges on either side. Linda lives with her boyfriend, George, and one of her sorority sisters whose nickname is Swiss. Swiss looks like the girl from the Swiss Miss hot chocolate package—long blond hair she could put into braids if she wanted, thin nose and lips.

My parents help me move my things into my dorm room on the sixth floor. The floors are bare, but my father has brought carpet he will roll out wall to wall then cut around our beds and desks with a box cutter. My dad feels awkward because my roommate is a black girl from the Bronx and he wants to turn on the O. J. Simpson trial while he's working on the carpet, wants an update. He's been watching the coverage religiously in the basement. He's been taking notes on yellow leg pads, pretending to be a juror, seeing what kind of verdict he would come up with. He is retired from the factory now, so he has time for this, is diving into it full-time like a job. My mother is still working at Anchor, determined to squeeze out as many years as she can, to pad her pension. She wants to earn more than Dad.

After my parents leave campus and I'm unpacking the rest of my bags and boxes, I find the paper where I've written down Dina's dorm building and room number. Of course she's in the nicer freshman dorm with air-conditioning. I see that my roommate has already installed her phone on the wall. Before I go to find Dina, I think about calling John to tell him I've arrived—Polly said to call collect—but I decide to wait. The feeling of freedom is pulsing through me, a new kind of blood in my veins. I can go wherever I want, come back whenever I want.

The path to Dina's dorm is two brick-covered walkways and a tennis court. I try to walk there nonchalantly, but end up trotting. Dusk is beginning to settle in the city sky, and it's getting cooler. All around me, freshmen are saying goodbye to their parents, and the air is buzzing with the collective energy of hundreds of eighteen-year-olds who want to drink, smoke cigarettes, have sex, get high, play songs with explicit lyrics at high volume. I hear Nine Inch Nails coming from an open window on the first floor of Dina's building. *I want to fuck you like an animal. I want to feel you from the inside.*

Dina's building is coed by wing, one side male, one female. My building is coed by floor, every other one girls, every other one boys, so we have quicker access to men through the stairwells when we want, and vice versa.

Dina has already made friends with a group of boys and when I arrive at her door, they are facing one another—Dina sitting on her bed, which is covered in a purple-flowered comforter, the boys sitting on the other bed, which is bare for now. Dina's roommate hasn't shown up yet (lucky again) and she'll end up with the room to herself for the first semester. She's Dina, after all. She's used to fortunate things coming to her.

The boys say they know of a bar downtown that will serve anybody, and we can probably just walk right in. Dina and I are still getting reacquainted, having spent all of high school not even remotely orbiting in the same circles. I feel a little uneasy about resuming our friendship.

Dina's not so much an ex-friend, but more like an ex-lover. My feelings for her are a deep well and I'm not quite ready to dive in, to lower my heart like a small wooden bucket she will undoubtedly fill with something. With her around, I'm always the less pretty one. Drinking together might help, though. The last time we drank together was from the Elvis bottles in my basement more than four years ago.

The boys lead us to a dive bar called Ruckus. There are five of us—three boys and me and Dina. I didn't catch any of their names. They are all Zack Morris types from *Saved by the Bell*—preppie, clean cut, their hair groomed, their clothes from Structure and

The Gap. We walk right in and grab a table, order two pitchers of mixed drinks—one Alabama Slammer, which is red, one Kamikaze, slightly green.

I make a joke about playing "red light, green light" with the drinks, remember Linda holding up Ping-Pong paddles in the backyard, pretending to be a traffic cop. Nobody laughs, and I begin to wonder if I've even said anything out loud. If I opened my mouth and only ash came out. The drinks taste like warm candy, go down clean and fast until the pitchers are empty and we walk the few sloping blocks back to campus.

We decide to ride the elevator in my building, which has fifteen floors. We aren't going anywhere in particular. We're drunk and need entertainment, something to do. One of the boys says something funny and I laugh so hard I fall to my knees. Dina picks me up, whispers in my ear, *stop being so dramatic,* but I can't help it. The mixture of alcohol and freedom in my system is devastating. I've never felt so unhinged.

We've lost track of time—no one has a watch, but eventually it feels like time to turn in. I push the button for floor six and it lights up like a warning. I say goodbye to Dina and the boys, who are likely glad to be rid of me so they can focus on fighting over Dina's attention.

I return to my room, where my roommate, Tamara, is in shorty pajamas, as my mother calls them. She's got her hair covered in a scarf, sitting on her bed on her side of the room reading a book. "Some *guy* has been calling for you all night," she says, her eyes boring holes in my face. I crumple onto my bed.

"Oh, must be my boyfriend, John. What did he say?"

"He just kept asking where you were," she says. "Sounded pissed off." She closes the book and peels back her sheets, which are deep purple. I wish they were mine. My mother bought beige sheets for my bed. A coral-colored comforter and blanket. My bed is ugly.

"You know, I have a boyfriend back in New York," Tamara says. "He goes to Fordham, full scholarship. He doesn't have time to waste stalking me." She folds herself into her bed, clicks off the little lamp she's clamped to her headboard.

I'm drunk and overheated, and the room stifling, no breeze from the tiny open window. The box fan is pushing hot air around the room, invisible cyclones of humidity I can feel on my skin. My stomach lurches. I need water, fresh air. I have neither.

I grab the phone off the wall, stretch it into the hallway, close the door, sit down on the floor. Out here in this narrow space, girls are walking to the community bathroom, carrying plastic shower baskets and toothbrushes. One girl has some sort of facial mask product on her face, bright green, like the rind of a lime, her skin only visible around her eyes, as if she's cut holes from the green to look out from.

I pull my father's calling card from my ID holder, his name in gold raised letters. It's for emergencies. As far as I can tell, I'm having one right now. I have no idea what time it is as I dial John's number. I'm not calling collect, don't think it's appropriate at this hour. I know John will answer. I'm not surprised by his voice, which has jagged edges. He is crying. It's not the first time I've heard him like this. In high school, I would try to break up with him, tell him I just wanted some time to be alone. There weren't other guys. I don't think any other boys in high school would have come near me. John's nickname on the football team was "Pyscho" for a reason. During these conversations, John would sob. He'd punch walls, punch himself in the face until I agreed to change my mind.

On the phone now, I feel that familiar tug on my insides, that feeling of nausea I get when he acts this way. He doesn't speak for what feels like a long time. We're just breathing to each other over this phone line, this slightly fuzzy connection—him in his bedroom in the country, where he can piss through the window screen if he wants to, me on the floor of this hallway on this campus in this shiny city.

John makes a heaving noise, gagging. He puts down the phone for a minute. I hear rustling through the holes in the phone's receiver. When I was a kid, I liked taking telephones apart, unscrewing the mouthpiece, a perfect round, examining the parts inside, those mechanisms that carry voices. Always concerned with the breaking down of things, the dissection, the picking apart. John comes back to the phone, finally manages to say something. "I just threw up."

There will be other conversations like this throughout the academic year. The last one will feature John's voice echoing as he tells me how he can't live without me, he won't live without me. It will sound like he's talking into a large plastic cup, like the Tupperware tumblers my mother used to make lemonade in. John will say he's got the barrel of his hunting rifle in his mouth. "I hope you're happy," he'll say and I'll feel sick again, sick all over this time, because I will be. Happy, that is.

★ ★ ★

Dina is my ticket to a world where I don't belong. A world where pretty girls get anything they want. We go to frat parties where people are charged five dollars for a plastic cup to drink beer from, but someone decides that Dina can get in free. Since I'm her sidekick, I slide through, too.

We go to the Oakland neighborhood of Pittsburgh and dance at a club called Zelda's, where they only ask to see a university ID for entrance, not a driver's license. We get men to buy us Sex on the Beach in fat glass tumblers, shots of who-knows-what in skinny glass test tubes, the colorful liquids glowing in black light, women in shorts and tank tops carrying the vials on their round trays, chemical waitresses, cash stuffed in their waistbands.

I get drunk and start telling everyone I encounter that Zelda was my grandmother's name, think that it's somehow fascinating to talk about your dead grandma at a nightclub over the blare of dance music thumping through large black speakers that line the walls.

In the bathroom, girls pee and put on makeup, adjust their hair in the water-stained mirrors. I only have two things in my pocket—a tube of lipstick and my school ID. I don't need money when I go out with Dina. Men buy us drinks and food, cigarettes, even drugs if we want them.

I pull the lipstick from my jeans and try my best to steady my hand as I put it to my lips. I'm blotting the excess with a stiff brown paper towel when a drunk girl opens the bathroom door, pushes another drunk girl in, then lets the door slam.

She is crying, this girl who's been pushed inside the bathroom against her will, and she moves to one of the toilets and starts throwing up violently. The other girls in the bathroom scurry out, but I stay, brave from the Sex on the Beach and the Fuzzy Navels and the Long Island Iced Teas, drinks that sound fun and adventurous, drinks that are served cold but burn your throat on the way down.

I lean over the puking girl, rub her back in small circles, say "Shhhhh, it's okay." When the wave of vomit subsides, she looks at me, her eyes black rings of wet eyeliner and mascara.

"I miss my mom," the girl says.

"I know," I say. And because we're both drunk and I believe she won't really understand me, won't remember my words, I add, "Me, too."

★ ★ ★

Throughout the first semester at college, Dina and I remain friends. We eat meals together in the dining hall, and Dina teaches me how to eat less and less, how to avoid gaining the freshman fifteen that many of the girls are talking about. Dina won't let me touch the fried foods, which are always available—french fries and onion rings and chicken fingers, breaded and hardened to a dark brown crisp.

Instead we pluck foil-wrapped baked potatoes from the baked potato bar, split them open, then top them with cottage cheese instead of sour cream. We eat dry salad because salad dressing makes you fat. We don't order the four-dollar pizzas from Corleone's, don't summon the delivery guy on his red ten-speed bicycle, which seems to be perpetually parked in front of the dorms at night.

With Dina, it's all about presentation. We can't appear to be silly little freshman girls, doing silly little freshman things, even though this is what I want the most. I want to talk too loud and laugh too much and act like a fool and realize that I don't know a damn thing about the world.

I want to throw myself into the wild, the wilderness of not-a-child-not-an-adult-either. Dina wants to go to aerobics classes in the student fitness center and have her nails manicured by the Vietnamese women downtown. Dina doesn't want to go to parties and dance like Uma Thurman's character in *Pulp Fiction*, fingers in a V-shape shimmying over her eyes. I want to do all these things, and I eventually find a girl on the floor of my dorm who wants to do them with me.

Her name is Janie and she has naturally curly hair and lips that are incredibly full and luscious even without lip liner or lipstick. I start pulling away from Dina and falling in love with Janie sometime around Thanksgiving, and by the time we return to school from holiday break in January, Janie and I are inseparable. We stay up all night together in her room having impossibly intricate conversations about anything we can think of. We don't really have to think of things to talk about, actually, as the words just keep springing furiously from our mouths.

Janie and I stumble to the dining hall for breakfast at 6:00 a.m., stack our plates with waffles and pancakes, then flood them with sweet maple syrup dispensed from a magical well, warm rivers of translucent amber. We eat as much as we want and drink thin black coffee that doesn't manage to keep us awake. Afterward, we climb into Janie's bed together, fall asleep with hands tangled in each other's hair, until her roommate wakes us for our classes, which luckily don't begin until the afternoon. We float by the rest of the day in a trancelike state, until we can retreat back to our girl den and start things all over—words and laughter and what seems to be more like love than anything I ever felt with anyone else in my entire world of nineteen years.

In high school, when John would notice me starting a friendship with a girl, he would call me a dyke. If I talked about spending the night at a girl's house, someone from marching band, John would tell me that if I went, then it definitely meant I was a lesbian. I used to think it might be true, was afraid that he knew something about me that I didn't.

Now, when Janie and I crawl into her twin-size bed after breakfast, I remember John's taunts and suddenly realize why he told me those lies, why my mother became angry when I started getting close to girls my age. They were both afraid of the power I'd find with girls, and they had good reason to. For now I feel the muscle of being a girl around other girls, of living in girl time—girl days, girl months, girl years. It's tunneling through my center, an electrical current that makes me feel as though I can do anything.

★ ★ ★

We're in my blue Subaru, me and Janie and Janie's roommate, Liz. I'm driving us to a fraternity party at another university in Pittsburgh, one with a mostly male enrollment, well known for engineering, computer sciences, and math, male-dominated fields of study.

Linda has warned me that parties on this campus are disappointing, overpopulated with two basic groups of men—ugly nerds and alpha-male brats. The male to female ratio at this school is five to one, which is why the fraternities at this college advertise their parties at other campuses in the city.

They want to attract girls, fresh meat. It's an expensive private school, so many of the students are already rich and will end up with high-paying scientific jobs to boot, and I wonder if I might find myself a wealthy husband at this party, an heir to some banking fortune perhaps, the fate my mother has always wanted for me.

The car I'm driving is the same one I drove in high school, a used sedan my father bought for me. It's a boxy little car, cigarette burns in the backseat, and the steering wheel shakes if you take it above 50 mph, but when the three of us are inside, the windows cracked and Alanis Morissette or No Doubt blaring from the small radio speakers, the car is alive, and breathing, our chariot of fire.

We arrive at the party, which is in a shabby-looking house off-campus. There are couches and ashtrays on the porch, a broken window on the second floor. It's February cold, the icy kind of cold that freezes our breath and makes us run from the car to the front door. We've left our coats at the dorm, have decided they aren't sexy.

There's no need to knock, we just open the door and walk right in. We pass through the living room, then the kitchen, where the sound of glasses clinking reminds me of wind chimes. We follow the thumping of bass to find the stairwell, slowly make our way downstairs.

At this party, like most house parties, the action is mostly happening in the basement, where the main lights are out and only a few strands of multicolored Christmas tree lights are guiding our way to the keg, the stack of bright red plastic cups, the makeshift dance floor.

It's not crowded like the parties at fraternity houses near our campus, which are mostly wall-to-wall sweaty bodies you have to weave around to get to the beer. There is plenty of room down here, and as our eyes begin to adjust and we take in our surroundings, we realize that the men outnumber the women two to one easily. We try to give one another looks that convey our excitement, but it's difficult to see faces in this near darkness.

Janie is our leader in most situations, so Liz and I follow her as she makes a few laps around the room, which is her custom at a party. Janie, like the Cher Horowitz character in the movie *Clueless*, believes one shouldn't commit to a location at a party until one has made at least two laps. You have to give yourself time to feel a party out. Most of the guys are lined up along the edges of the cement-block walls, drinking beer from their cups.

The music is deafening, making it impossible to talk, so we make faces at one another, mime out messages, and generally have no idea what we're trying to say, but it doesn't matter, because Nine Inch Nails is blasting and soon Janie spies our target—a group of three guys in one of the corners of the room—and she leads the way for our landing.

Trent Reznor sings *Bow down before the one you serve, you're going to get what you deserve.* The song is "Head Like a Hole" and now I'm the one against the wall, a boy's body rubbing against me as we sway in time to the music, a boy's mouth on mine, lips opening and closing. His hands are on my waist and my hands are running through his hair and we have no idea who we are at this point, can't even really see ourselves or anyone else in the room, but the beer and the melody and the strands of lights make it okay to use our bodies like this, okay because I do deserve this, this reaching for a stranger so desperately.

On the way home, my lips feel swollen, and buzzing with sound, as if my mouth has its own frequency now. I'm a little tipsy, but believe I'm okay to drive. Then somehow I make a wrong turn and we are lost in Wilkinsburg, a mostly unsavory section of the city we've been told to avoid, especially at night. I think we should stop for directions, even though it's 2:00 a.m. and the only open establishment we pass is a beleaguered little convenience store, out-of-service gas pumps quietly rotting in front.

I think of Elizabeth Bishop's "Filling Station," a poem we recently read in my Principles of English Literature class, along with mystical verses by Rumi and an unsettling poem about a dead duchess. "Filling Station" describes a grease-soaked gas station with grease-soaked workers, a family operation. The speaker of the poem notices the contrast of the filth with the carefully arranged oil cans, the dainty doilies draped sweetly over the dirty mess, small signs of light among the dark.

My professor is a grad student, an honest woman with short blond hair and round glasses. I feel something like lightning along my spine as she discusses the significance of the poem's final line: *Somebody loves us all.* After class she stops me, smiles and says, "You really get it. I can tell."

I'm not sure I know what *it* is, only know that I am happiest when words are nearby, swishing in my brain or jumping from pages like the pop-up books I used to covet at the Carnegie Library in Connellsville. You weren't able to check them out. They were *non-circulating,* according to the librarian, so I could only sit at the low Formica tables and delicately turn the pages, watch them bloom into landscapes, two dimensions transforming into three before my very eyes.

We sit inside the car in the parking lot of the convenience store for a few minutes, attempt to analyze our situation, which would be easier without beer in our systems. Janie, who is tall like me, is sitting in the passenger seat, and Liz, who is barely five feet even in her thick heeled boots, is in the back, lunged over the center console like a kid on a family trip.

Liz says something to the effect of *You are not getting out of this car, don't even think about it.* Liz is from Pittsburgh, lives near the Heinz plant, the factory sign a neon red ketchup bottle pouring neon red letters H-E-I-N-Z out one by one, over and over again. Liz knows the city, knows we don't belong here at this place at this time, says she can get us back to campus if she can just have a minute to think, to shake the drink out of her brain.

Janie double-checks the door locks and makes sure all the windows are rolled up, then slides down in her seat a little. I turn to see her face, the look of uncertainty I'm not used to noticing in her features.

Her eyes get wide as if she's just seen a ghost behind me and when I turn my head to look left out the driver's-side window, I see an old woman with a patch of black whiskers growing from her chin leaning in close, her hands fashioned into fleshy binoculars over her eyes so she can see inside the car.

When we try to ignore her, all three of us looking straight ahead like girl statues, Liz whispers from the backseat *"Fucking drive, Karen!"* The old woman knocks on the glass with the knuckle of her index finger, as if she's calling on a neighbor, rapping on their door to borrow a cup of sugar. We let out a collective scream now, and I put the car in drive, my foot on the gas.

After a few minutes of circling the same block several times, Liz remembers where we need to go, and when we finally pull into a parking space near our dorm, it feels like survival. We're so glad to be alive we nearly shout it from the tiny window.

The next morning, it's the old woman with the whiskers we remember. We'll talk about her as if she wished to harm us, cook us in a giant pot the way a storybook witch would. And the boys whose bodies we rubbed against won't even be part of the fable. We didn't need them after all, having followed our own breadcrumbs home.

★ ★ ★

When I go home for the summer after my first year at college, the house is a museum. There should be a velvet rope across the entrance to my bedroom. A perfect example of a girl's sleeping quarters from the 1990s. A pink diorama, a still life with a *Reality Bites* movie poster. Linda is staying at her Pittsburgh apartment for a few more weeks, finishing out her part-time job at the cosmetics counter at Kaufmann's, the downtown department store with a glass elevator and two restaurants.

It's just the three of us right now—my parents and me. My mother has moved herself into the other room in the basement, has dragged the double bed from Linda's room down there. The basement has its own door to the outside, becomes Mother's studio apartment. She can come and go as she pleases.

My father, retired from Anchor for three years now, is back to work at a different factory, Sony Electronics in Mt. Pleasant. He works an assembly line where they make bar codes for the various Sony products, rolls of bar codes he must handle with special gloves because they are sensitive to heat and the warmth from his hands might interfere with hidden messages inside the black lines and numbers.

I have a temporary job working at that same plant for the summer, but they put me in a different department. I'm in a large drafty room where we prep picture tubes for 32-inch television sets. I work twelve-hour night shifts, 7:00 p.m. to 7:00 a.m. I eat one turkey sandwich a day all summer long—two slices of bread, one slice of turkey, and a dollop of mustard smeared with a butter knife from a glass jar. Plastic squeeze bottles of condiments are blasphemy in our house. *Only the best comes in glass.* I cut the sandwich in half diagonally, eat half when I wake up in the afternoon, the other half before I go to sleep around 8:00 a.m.

The chubby women who work with me in the picture tube room tell me to eat on my breaks, but I only smoke cigarettes, the long and slender kind that I think are more elegant, all the men flirting with me, fighting over who gets to light me up. I'm the only young woman in the department, an exotic among the natives.

I've set out to shed what bit of the freshman fifteen I gained from the pancake and waffle breakfasts, the 3:00 a.m. walks with

Janie and Liz to the all-night McDonald's next to Point State Park. We'd eat mounds of french fries, dip them in our hot fudge sundaes. We'd be the youngest people there, the other customers at that hour a mix of old homeless men and women and veterans who drank coffee and panhandled outside with ragged cardboard signs.

I whittle myself down quickly, between the one sandwich a day and the 111 leg lifts and the 111 sit-ups, the old routine I've resurrected in my bedroom at night. I try not to breathe too heavily, don't want my father to ask what on earth I'm doing. My mother is in her basement cocoon, she has no idea, disconnected from the rest of us, as if our family is an electrical outlet and she's simply unplugged herself, removed herself from the power source.

When Linda joins us in July, my mother makes no apologizes for the missing bed in her room. Linda sleeps on the floor in my room, propped up on pillows. We watch the 1996 Summer Olympics every night. They're taking place in the United States this year, in Atlanta. I'd done a presentation on the Olympics in IMPACT in fourth grade, remember researching the history of the games in Greece, remember the rituals of the torch, the symbolism, how the interlocking color rings represent the five continents, how it reminded me of my family, the five of us, two parents and three sisters. You can separate us by miles, but we'll still remember where we came from.

I've always told myself that nothing bad can happen in the world during the Olympics, the entire world united through this fourteen-day event. I cried as I watched fireworks on TV during the closing ceremonies in Calgary, the 1988 Olympic Games, because I knew that once the games were over, people would start murdering each other again. I believe the Olympics could keep the world safe.

But my theory is proven wrong in Atlanta, in 1996, as Linda and I watch the news coverage of the bombing at Centennial Park. It's not the first time I've heard "America" and "terrorism" in the same sentence.

I remember the Oklahoma City bombing from last year. When I was a kid, terrorists were people who lived in other countries, like Libya, far-off places that couldn't touch me. Now, terror seems to be walking all around. Now, mass murderers are coming up with more efficient ways to kill people. Sonny and his gun at the factory feels almost primitive. These days, he would have just blown up the entire place.

Women's gymnastics is my favorite event. I like watching the girls in their tight leotards, their smooth childlike bodies running and flipping during the floor exercises, catapulting between uneven parallel bars, their hands and arms white with chalk. There's always a box of Twinkies in the house. Linda eats them slowly as we watch gymnastics. Linda has a method. She breaks a Twinkie in half, digs all the cream filling out with her tongue, then eats the spongy cake. I eat one triangle of turkey and mustard sans bread, getting high on the smell of sugar in the room, the girls without breasts tumbling through the screen.

Now that I'm back in Connellsville, I'm also back with John, although I won't say that he's my boyfriend again, won't put that name to it, even in my mind. It's as though my body had left its shape here, as if I was cut out of the scene with scissors when I left, a paper doll. When I return, the space is still there for me to fit inside, the outline of my edges thick and black. I click into place like a missing puzzle piece. I make the picture complete again.

It's summer on the Banks family farm, which has always been my favorite time. We ride the quad out through the cornfields, John's hunting rifle strapped to my back. When John spies a groundhog, he stops, kills the engine, and I must be quiet like Elmer Fudd out hunting Bugs Bunny. John's Pap is offering him ten dollars for every groundhog he can kill this summer, says they are ruining the fields, ruining the crops.

I see the animal in the distance, how it stands on its hind legs like a trained circus pet. When John shoots, the animal is knocked down, a target at a carnival game, but this is real, this is a life. I cry for the animals, their bloated bodies John throws into black trash bags. "Don't be such a baby," he says. "They are pests."

I say small prayers for the dead as we drive back to the trailer, even though I've no idea who I'm praying to.

The cows on the farm live in the fenced-in field that runs adjacent to the gravel lane I drive on to reach the Banks family trailer. They are milk cows and as far as I know they won't be killed for meat, only attached to shiny metal milking machines inside the barn. Still, I worry for them and wonder if they know something of their fate, their lot in life. Do they ever wonder why they are here, the way I still wonder why I was born in a specific place and time, imagine how my life would be different if I were somebody or something else?

I'm driving down the lane one late summer morning, on my way to pick up John so we can go fishing at Green Lick Dam, something we do to pass the time on my days off, to get me out of the museum house, out of Mother's way. The sun is hanging above the green hill, as if nailed to the sky, an object of art on a light blue wall. There is dew on the grass the cows trample over. Their legs mechanical, they are spotted machines.

I suddenly get the urge to see a cow up close, so I press the brakes, throw the Subaru in park, and get out. I walk over to the fence, to a single cow who appears to be waiting patiently for me. I look into her eyes and they are more like mine than I wish to know, but I'm afraid to look away, so I don't. We are a girl and a cow. We are both animals, both wanting the same thing.

Every August a sick back-to-school feeling creeps up in my throat, and this year is no different. John isn't going back to community college. He's working at an auto parts store in town, has been promised a manager's position if he sticks with it. He wants me to quit school, too, get a place with him. He'll take care of me. This is what we talk about the nights we play pool together at the pool hall, balancing cue sticks with cigarettes between our fingers, shooting 8-ball. I am stripes. John is solids.

"If you go back to school, then you don't love me," John says between long drags of smoke, but I know it's not as simple as that, not some equation I can solve. *If x equals stay, then you love me.* I don't know if I love John, although I still answer *I love you, too* when we hang up the phone each night, still go through our years-old routine of call and response.

I don't know how to reach for the feelings I have for John, just like I don't know how to reach for the feelings I have for my mother. When I do, it's like putting my hand in a bowl of fishhooks. I can't pick up just one. My feelings for them are hopelessly tangled, love hooked on memory hooked on family hooked on pain.

There are no sure signs of love—I know this now. When I was a kid the sign was this: You picked a yellow flower called a buttercup, and you held it under your chin. If your skin reflected the color of the flower, it meant you were in love. But as I grew I realized it was just a trick—the skin can't help but reflect the color of those slick yellow petals. Love can't help but be in us all.

★ ★ ★

I am going back to college, so I'm halfway inside the pink closet of my pink bedroom, digging around for shoes. I'm home alone for now, Mother and Father at their factories, Linda at the Valley Dairy Restaurant near the banks of the Yough River downtown. She's been waitressing there all summer, saving all of her tips in a plastic shower bucket she keeps under her bed. I count her money often, but stop short of peeling five dollar bills from the thick wad for myself, although the idea is tempting.

I walk into my parents' bedroom, where my father sleeps alone now, his threadbare blue pajamas he wears every night folded neatly on his pillow. I pick them up to smell them, breathe in a scent that reminds me of childhood—a mix of gold Dial soap and Barbasol shaving cream.

I open up the wicker chest at the foot of the bed, that treasure chest of keepsakes. I dig through the fat stacks of photographs, the school artwork, the newspaper clippings, some laminated for safe-keeping, some yellowed and threatening to disintegrate with the warmth of touch.

My body knows what I'm looking for, but my mind pretends to have forgotten. That thin medical file, the pediatrician's observation notes scrawled inside. I want to find it again, so I can keep it for myself, to know that it was real.

I am still digging for it, removing the contents of the chest, heaps of history piling up around me. I am on my knees, searching. Before I know it the entire chest is empty, but I haven't found the manila folder, my name on the tab, last name first, first name last. It's gone. My mind can explain it away like a ghost, but my body remembers.

I never told anyone about the medical file, not John or Linda or Pam. I never asked my parents about it, and I never will. I want it to remain a secret, but I also want it to be my secret. I wish I could have it all to myself now. I wish I could study those two pages, analyze the doctor's handwriting. I wish I could know what day of the week it was in 1980 when I was examined. I wish I could know these details, yet I'm afraid to know anything more. I'm afraid of the darkness that will surely spill from me otherwise. Not asking about it means my mind can keep its distance from my body. My mind will remain safe in this orderly world I've created. My mind will pretend not to hear the whispers of my body.

# CHAPTER 28

# Ten for a Bird

Another year of college has sent me spinning, a ballerina in a music box dancing toward words. There will never be enough time to read all the books I want to read, and that fact both thrills me and scares me. Time is a heart ticking in my chest.

Home for the summer again, it's 1997. The world here has mostly stayed where I put it when I left in the fall. The town that time forgot. I sleep with a stack of novels and poetry collections on top of my nightstand, keep candy bars hidden in the top drawer, where I also hide the empty wrappers. Linda has graduated from college. She's home for good now, my father unloading a U-Haul full of her apartment things into the basement.

My mother walks around the house like her skin is constantly itching, on fire. She doesn't want Linda here. I took a psychology course last semester, learned about manic depression, episodes of mania and depression, moods swinging like a weight tied to a rope. My professor, a tall kind woman with salt and pepper hair, mentioned the work of Kay Redfield Jamison, a psychiatrist who documented her own diagnosis with manic depression in a book called *An Unquiet Mind: A Memoir of Moods and Madness*. I jotted the title down in my notebook, then bought a copy of the book, gave it to my mother as a birthday gift in March. It sits in the magazine rack unread, under stacks of *Good Housekeeping* and *Redbook,* the bibles on womanhood I read as a child to learn about the world.

I am back with John again, the rubber band between us still intact even though it's thinning, all that stretching out then snapping back. John has quit his job at the auto parts store, says it was because of me, the stress I caused him when I was away. He doesn't do much of anything now but beg beer money from his parents and follow me around. When I'm not working my summer job at The Variety Store, we drive around in his black Chevy Cavalier that smells too much like little tree air freshener.

There is sex again, John still believing he is my first and only. I don't tell him that I've had sex with other men at college this past year, even though he pushes me for this information regularly, as though he knows the truth and only wants to trick me into saying it. There's also his family again, his little sister Katie who is almost three years old now. Katie squeals when she sees me for the first time in months. She remembers my name, but can't say her *R* sounds, calls me *Kawen.*

My father is still working nights at Sony. My mother usually goes to sleep right after Dad leaves, but tonight she's milling around the house. We hear her going up and down the basement steps. We hear the front door open and close a few times. She's been colder than usual lately, her eyes more vacant, her shoulders slightly slumped as though she's exhausted from carrying the weight of her body for fifty-five years.

After the U-Haul is unpacked and our father at work, Linda and I set up shop in my bedroom to watch TV. Then we go out to the kitchen so Linda can retrieve her Twinkies, pour herself a tall glass of milk. Our mother appears in the entryway, standing at the threshold where dining room carpet meets kitchen linoleum.

"I'm leaving," she says. It's as simple as that. Just one sentence. Just two words.

Linda has emptied the milk jug, bubbles on the surface of her full glass bursting in the air one by one. If she's surprised by our mother's announcement, I'm not sure why. For the last two weeks, every time my mother left for work, she took a large black trash bag with her, presumably full of donations to Goodwill. When she'd return home after her shift, the bag would be gone, but the Goodwill donation drop-off is nowhere between our house and the factory. We haven't spoken about it, but I thought that Linda knew what was going on. I must have been wrong.

Now Linda slams her fist down on the kitchen counter. She says nothing, at first, just throws the empty milk jug at my mother's face. Mother doesn't duck in time, a move that appears to be intentional, like she's bracing herself for the inevitable firing squad. Linda runs down the hall, yelling "Mothers aren't the ones who are supposed to leave! We are!" I hear the bottom of my bedroom door grazing the carpet as it closes, the shag too high for the door to slam as quickly as Linda would like it to right now.

My mother and I are alone in the kitchen, the empty milk jug at her feet, tears as big as raindrops in her eyes. She opens her arms to me silently, reaching for me, but I don't go to her. I pick up a Twinkie and unwrap it, shove it into my mouth in one piece, the cream filling coating my throat on the way down. I eat a second, then a third this way, until my mother finally lowers her arms and turns around, walks out the front door.

★ ★ ★

At work, Mary is teaching me how to count money. Of course I already know how to count money, but because Mary is nearly eighty years old, she has a special method. She insists I follow her order, which is pennies first. She counts the pennies, then records their total value on a scrap of register tape. Then she counts the nickels and follows the same procedure. Then dimes, quarters, and paper money (dollar bills first, naturally). Then she adds the long column of numbers. The most frustrating part for me is Mary uses a pencil so dull, the point is barely visible. My pencils must be razor sharp. In elementary school I kept a tiny manual sharpener at my desk, often using it between paragraphs if I had to.

Mary's entire counting process takes about fifteen minutes. She advises me not to count in my head, and demands I show my work. "If you don't write it down, you're just asking for carelessness," she warns, her voice gravelly, thick with phlegm she must cough regularly into a tissue. I watch with feigned interest as Mary tenderly slides each stack of wrinkled paper bills out of the plastic till. Who in their right mind counts pennies first? Pennies, the lowest value and therefore least important in the currency hierarchy, should obviously be counted last. Pennies are dirty. And they have a nasty habit of turning black and gummy over time.

I am stuck working in this store for the summer. It's called, simply, The Variety Store, and I suppose it earns its name. We sell toys, power tools, light bulbs, hearing aid batteries, paint, bar soap, and ballpoint pens, among other things. We will copy any key for you while you wait and cut you some very ugly linoleum or outdoor carpeting off a giant roll. We use X-Acto knives for this purpose, which we keep in the pockets of our blue smocks.

When there aren't customers waiting to check out at the register, there are things to keep me busy. I can clean the entryway rugs. This process involves spraying blue window cleaner on the surface of the rug, then sweeping a stiff corn broom across it from side to side. I can observe the shelves. The store manager, Janet, a woman in her mid-forties with thick glasses, wants me to get to know the merchandise, so she sends me out to roam the aisles. When she catches me straightening up the LEGO shelf she chides me. "I just want you to look. No straightening. That's Kelly's job."

There are only four employees here all together: Mary, Janet, Kelly, and me. Kelly is thirtyish, with a severe perm and beige foundation. Her main job is to straighten and dust the shelves and help customers find things. My main job is to ring people up and cut keys, a process Janet taught me on day one. I have to wear giant safety goggles when I use the key cutter, and desperately hope no one I know ever walks in the store to witness me in them.

In spite of the eyewear, the key machine is my favorite part of the job. First, you select the correct blank. If it's a car key, you need to know the make. Let's say it's Ford. Now you need to look closely on the neck of the customer's original key. There is a tiny letter etched there. That's how you know which blank to use. I like the authority the key-making process grants me, examining the key then plucking the appropriate blank from the revolving rack while the customer watches, playing the concerned patient to my know-it-all surgeon. Then I don my protective gear, the giant goggles and sandpapery gloves. The original key goes in a vise. The machine traces it, remembering its pattern when I pass the blank through. Finally, I get to use a nifty little buffing device to rid the key of any excess metal clumps.

The buffer spins and spins, the key making a little screeching sound with each touch. If you buff for too long, you'll ruin the key and sparks will fly, hence the glasses. Mary has already warned me of this, even though Janet hasn't allowed her anywhere near the key cutter for the last five years.

"Dee-men-sha," Janet mouths to me behind Mary's back one afternoon as Mary packs up her things to leave. She always wears one of those thick plastic rain bonnets—transparent, flat on top— even when it's not raining.

The Variety Store is part of a large complex called Pechin Shopping Village. Pechin's is a local legend here, serving the area for more than fifty years. The "village" is actually a system of flat, tar-roofed buildings built one right next to the other. The buildings aren't connected from inside; they each have their own entrances. In the center, cars are lined up like sardines in a giant parking lot, and most days it's filled to capacity.

There's the grocery, with slanted floors and displays made out of cut-up cardboard boxes; the deli, famous for double-scoop ice-cream cones that only cost a quarter; the sporting goods store, a sea of bright orange hunting coats, rubbery camouflage vests, and stiff mesh caps with safety pins for attaching your fishing license; the clothing store, mostly elastic-waist polyester pants and orthopedic shoes that look like bricks; the bakery, home of delicious ten-cent donuts and no air-conditioning; The Variety Store; and, of course, the cafeteria.

It's the same cafeteria where Sonny had coffee with co-workers in 1985 before he went on his killing spree at Anchor. On my lunch break, I look around at the dirty tables, wonder where the men were sitting on that day, and the ticking of my heart nearly stops when I realize it was already twelve years ago. Oh, twelve, oh, eleven. Two of my favorite numbers, those ages when I tried to control the world, make it fall out of orbit. Even though I'm twenty years old now, I still take eleven sips from every water fountain I use. I still run my toothbrush under the faucet six times, back and forth like a magic wand casting a spell on the flowing water.

If you don't mind whirring industrial fans and flies that look like they belong in the Amazon, you can go to Pechin's cafeteria and enjoy delicacies like twenty-cent hamburgers and ninety-nine-cent manicotti dinners (complete with garlic bread and a small salad).

It's August again and there's that lazy end of summer glow on everything that makes me nervous. The novelty of the job has worn off and our clientele manage to depress me more and more each day.

Customers come in without wearing shoes. They come in looking like they just stepped out of Dunbar Creek, mud collected around their ankles. They come in angry, looking for a certain size screw that doesn't exist, forcing me to scour the hardware aisle with them, pulling every damn screw out of every damn box so we can discover that none are a match.

It's been two weeks since my mother left. We haven't heard from her. No letters or phone calls, no sightings around town. The night she walked out, the backseat of her Lincoln stuffed with the last two garbage bags of her belongings, Linda wailed to our father on the phone. He called from work around 1:00 a.m., on his break, something he never does, because they don't have phones in his department at Sony. He has to walk all the way to the cafeteria to make calls and he only has ten minutes, his journey to the phone bank and back taking up his entire break. My father must have known what was happening. That's why he called.

"Daddy, she left!" Linda sobbed into the curved mauve mouthpiece. Mother recently redecorated our entire upstairs in the colors mauve and blue. Now there's a mauve and blue stained-glass picture hanging next to the front door. It's from Home Interiors and it says THERE'S NO PLACE LIKE HOME. "Can you come home, Daddy? Please come home!" Linda said. I grabbed the phone from her.

"We're fine," I said. I didn't want to upset him.

Two days after my mother left I was downstairs, sitting at my father's fly-making station, calming myself by going through his supplies, just like I used to do as a little girl. I ran my fingers over the feathers, the fake fur, the shiny spools of thread, the shiny little scissors. I looked up at his fishing calendar tacked to the wall. He likes to record details about every fishing trip—the time and location and the temperature of the water and the bait he used and how many fish he caught.

Each day's square is filled with this information written neatly in horizontal rows. The square for the day my mother left looks different. He's written something diagonally, in cursive script, not his usual blocky print. *Today was a very sad day.*

Now I'm at the cash register at The Variety Store and Mary's shift is finally over and I can count the money any damn way I please. I'm thinking about how I'll probably go over to John's house right after work and spend the night. His parents don't mind if I sleep over, even letting me share John's twin bed, as long as we keep the door open, our feet dangling over the side by morning. We are adults now, after all. My father doesn't worry about me driving down Route 982 anymore. Linda worries enough for all three of us now. She doesn't like being in the house alone when Dad works night shift, sleeps with all the lights on, a baseball bat leaning in the corner behind the bedroom door.

When I woke up this morning, Dad was out back, digging up the sod to make a small garden, destroying the perfect grass the landscapers put down so many years ago. He came inside and started cooking breakfast—rainbow trout and eggs. He kept the radio on while he cooked, left it on while he ate, too. "I'll just plant some tomatoes and cucumbers," he said. "It's late in the season, but I've got to start somewhere." We've all got to start somewhere.

I'm standing behind the cash register at The Variety Store, counting loose change from the pocket of my blue smock, trying to determine how many donuts I can buy on my break, when my mother walks through the door. She's in her work clothes—V-neck T-shirt, pressed jeans, her grease-stained purse hanging from her shoulder. She's smiling tentatively, as if she's approaching someone who may not know her and she's hoping she'll be recognized.

"I thought I'd come by and get an ice-cream cone," she says. "I heard they have really good ice cream here."

★ ★ ★

My mother and I are sitting on a bench in the parking lot outside Pechin deli, ice cream melting down the sides of our cones, making milky stains on the blacktop under our feet.

I look straight ahead to avoid looking at her face. If we lock eyes, I'll feel a thousand feelings at once, jagged edges of emotion seeping out of her skin. They must be invisible to everyone else, but I can see them and I have to look away.

She is all raw nerve, all corpuscle, which comes from the Latin *corpusculum,* meaning *small body.* Corpuscles are red and white blood cells, the basic components of matter or light. My mother is simply an element now, having broken herself down into the most rudimentary of parts.

"Will you come see my apartment sometime?" she asks. Her voice is a piece of tissue paper rustling in the wind. Like a child who feels she must pick a side between divorcing parents, I don't ever want to see my mother's apartment. I know she will see it as a victory over my father, me staying on my side of the line she's drawn between the middle of our family, the picking of teams in a kickball game. *It will always be me and you against Dad and Linda.* Her words from some of my earliest memories. *You're built just like me.* But that is no longer true, so what happens now? My mother has disassembled herself and I have worked to reconstruct myself, adding some parts, repurposing others to fit the way I want them to.

"Sure, I guess," is my reply, but I realize that I no longer have to answer her, that I can say and do whatever I want, a jolt of magnetic energy through my system. Maybe it's just the sugar from the ice cream, or the chemical rush of knowing that in ten minutes I will go back to my register at The Variety Store, and my mother will go back to her apartment, a place I imagine decorated in beige and lace, windows with frilly curtains.

It's a little like death, this pulling away, this mourning for some kind of loss. Tonight, at John's house, Polly will make me hot tea and hug me tighter than usual. Later, I'll lie in John's bed with him and cry myself to sleep, bury my face in his bare shoulder, make it slippery with my tears, but by morning I'll realize that I'm not mourning the loss of my mother. I'm mourning the loss of an origin, but even that doesn't feel true. For how can you mourn something you were never really certain existed?

# CHAPTER 29

# Not to Be Missed

My father and I are in my red Oldsmobile Cutlass Supreme. We are moving south on I-95 in Georgia, about to cross the Florida state line. There's a welcome center there, where you can get a Dixie cup of fresh orange juice, dry your hands with automatic dryers in the bathrooms, motion activated. We've made this drive before, usually with all four of us in the Town Car, the backseat big enough that Linda and I could both sleep there if we bent our bodies in half, our heads meeting in the middle. This time, it's just me and my father, driving to Pam and Allen's house, a cute little bungalow in St. Petersburg.

This time, we're not going for a visit. This time, I'm going there to live. My father is afraid of flying, will take a Greyhound bus back to Pennsylvania in a week, after I'm settled.

It's the middle of June 1999. I finished college about a month ago, a strained graduation ceremony where my mother acted like she'd been put together with Scotch tape, pieces of her threatening to fall off in the gymnasium, outside the reception hall, at the T.G.I. Friday's we went to for dinner afterward.

That night, after my parents and Linda left my off-campus apartment—where I'd lived alone, staying up most nights writing poems in a tie-dyed beanbag chair—I wanted to go out, maybe get a

251

drink, toast myself. Not that it had been that difficult to get a degree in English, but still, it was something. I thought there should be some kind of observance.

I called John and even though we hadn't talked for almost two years, having finally severed the veins between us for good, a knock-down-drag-out fight that lasted for weeks, so gory that I doubt neither of us will properly remember it, one of those memories the body blocks to protect the mind, he answered. In spite of it all, John showed up in his green Jetta, drove me to a bar three blocks from my apartment. The Great Escape, it was called.

He bought us each two shots of whiskey, devil water, and we clinked our stubby glasses together. Little Katie is five years old now, and when he shows me a snapshot of her from his wallet, a cute picture of her standing in a flower bed, a photo taken by Polly, a fantastic photographer who takes copious notes about every photo she snaps, writes extensive information on the back of each developed shot in her beautiful cursive writing, I feel a pang of sadness. Missing out on the girl's growing up. As if I should still be there, a girl-shaped hole in the Banks family waiting for me. But even if I wanted to, I know I no longer fit.

"Katie still talks about you," John says. "If she sees a picture of you, she'll ask, '*Where is my friend?*'" I laugh a little in the darkness of the bar, cover the hardness in my throat with another sip of whiskey.

I tell John about my plan to move to Florida. How I will live with Pam and Allen, get a job, save up money for my own place, perhaps a little apartment near the beach. "Or you could stick around to see how I turn out," he says, brushing my bare leg with his fingertips. I smile, drain my first glass, place it facedown on the bar like people do in the movies.

My mother lives in the same apartment she invited me to see two years ago, a one-bedroom in Connellsville above Duke's Bar, next to the Green Garden Miniature Golf course I loved as a child—the rickety windmill, the tiny sand traps, the final hole that is really a tunnel through which your ball disappears. In spite of her relentless messages on my answering machine, countless requests for me to visit, I still haven't been there.

It's been two years since my mother left my father. She's filed for divorce, but it's not final, my father choosing to refuse signing the paperwork. It will automatically become official after three years of inaction on his part, so that's what he'll wait for. He won't sign a damn thing.

When I visit him at the house on Washington, he has country music playing on the radio. He sings along, seems to know all the words to every song. I worry about him listening to such sad music, but he dances around the kitchen to it, spinning circles in his black leather slippers on the dingy floor. The house never smells like cleaning chemicals anymore, the baseboards not scrubbed for two years.

My mother took Midas and Veronica with her when she left, took Sybil Elaine to the animal shelter. She left Charmin and Honey Louise for my father, left a note about Sybil, didn't even tell him in person. My father called the shelter right away, rushed down there to get Sybil as soon as he could.

"Why did she have to go and do that? Take Sybil's mom away?" he'd asked me. The two cats had still been close, often sleeping together in white lumps, Veronica still grooming Sybil like she was still her kitten.

"Well, you know how she is," was my only response. It's become a mantra for the three of us—my father, Linda, and me. We know how Mother is and that is enough explanation. It sums up years of living with her, years of emptying of all those buckets under the sink, the accumulation of mother's sickness, her sadness, her moods I've been charting all of my life. Until now.

On I-95, when we stop at the Florida Welcome Center, my father says it's my turn to drive. He's taken us all this way. I can finish the job, driving almost the entire length of Florida down to Pinellas County. I don't know what I'll do down there, only know that Pam and Allen said I can stay in their extra bedroom, which is actually an attached single-car garage that's been converted into a real room. There's an aquarium in there, and I'll watch the fish at night, swimming through the glow. My Cutlass is packed to capacity. No furniture, just my computer, my books, clothes, shoes. I've left most of my possessions behind.

I drive us around Jacksonville, then through Starke, where Ted Bundy was executed in 1989. It's a small patch of nothing, the State Prison one of the only buildings in town. I drive us through Ocala, through Florida farmland, nothing like the Pennsylvania farms I'm used to, the rolling hills and pastures, the cows on the Banks family farm, those sacred animals that speak with their eyes, although they will never spill their secrets.

Everything is flat down here in Florida. You can make good time, travel faster. I drive through the city of Tampa, across the Howard Frankland Bridge that connects to St. Petersburg.

I've made a mix tape for the trip, and for the final thirty minutes of the drive, I keep rewinding, listening to the same song over and over. It's about 1:00 a.m., and my father and I are almost there, having decided to drive straight through instead of stopping halfway in Rock Hill, South Carolina, to stay overnight. We just want to get there.

I'm trying to keep my eyes open for these last few miles, my father next to me in the passenger seat with his shoes off, looking out the window at the lights reflecting off the water. The Howard Frankland Bridge is eleven miles long, "The Frankenstein" some of the local people call it, and when we finally cross it, we'll be only minutes from Pam's house.

The song I keep replaying is "Feels Like Home." It's a song written and recorded first by Randy Newman, but this rendition is sung by Chantal Kreviazuk. Her voice is a little ragged around the edges, sometimes small, sometimes swelling to crescendo in the chorus.

*Feels like home to me.*
*Feels like I'm all the way back where I come from.*

As the song ends and my hand reaches for the tape deck, the rewind button smooth from the touch of my fingertips over the years, my father turns to me.

"So, is this why you're coming down here?" he asks. "It feels like home?"

The cassette clicks to a stop.

I press play.

A piano intro swells the car with sound.

*If you knew how lonely my life has been. . . .*
*If you knew how I wanted someone to come along*
*and change my world. . . .*

I see the sign for our exit up ahead, emerald-green with white reflective letters that shine in the car's headlights. I don't answer my father, don't know what this place feels like just yet. There are so many unknowns, so many faces in the darkness, so many apparitions at the threshold of any room.

I click on my turn signal, merge from the bridge onto Fourth Street.

I roll down the window and allow the humid air to press its hands against my face, my throat.

There are so many pairs of hands out there, on factory floors in factory towns. Assembling vessels, assembling entire lives.

There is one thing I do know, and it rides with me, inside my body and my mind: I can rewrite the story of where I come from. Maybe get it right this time.

# Reading Group Guide

1. How did you react to the central image of the girl factory? In what ways are girls "built" and "assembled," as the author suggests?

2. Why does Karen's mother have so many superstitions or "Mother's ways" as her father calls them? What kind of effect do they have on the young Karen?

3. On page 5, Karen catalogs the different ways her father could die at the glass factory—heart attack, explosion, a fall into the furnace. Why do you think she is so afraid he will die?

4. On page 15, Karen writes "Some stories end. They end and exist in a space where things are final. They won't be told again because you've already learned from that story. You know what the story knows. But other stories, they never end. Instead, they continue to grow, continue to be told, the feelings in them felt over and over, a living, breathing part of you, an organ, like skin or a lung." What does she mean by this?

5. On page 23, Karen's mother says that superstitions are like insurance, acknowledging that "Sometimes you need to do certain things to make sure bad things won't happen. And other times you need to do certain things to give good things a helping hand." Do you believe this? Karen then says, "I can control the world by following these superstitions and by counting things." How does this help to give her a sense of control?

6. Why do you think Karen is so fascinated by weather and wants to be a meteorologist?

7. How did you react to the scene in Chapter 4 when Karen's mother catches her reaching the "dew point"? Why is she so angry? Why does Karen compare her mother to Sonny? Why is this such a pivotal scene? After reading the entire book, do you have a different

perspective on why her mother might have such a strong negative reaction?

8. Why does Karen's mother clean so often?

9. What do you think of Karen's relationship with her mother? How is it complicated? What is her opinion of her mother? She uses the word "superficial" to describe her mother on page 58 and she also alludes to the fact that her mother has a heart but doesn't know how to use it at the end of Chapter 8. Does this show that even as a child she knows something isn't quite right? How is your own relationship with your mother?

10. How are rituals and routines important in factory life, both at work and at home?

11. On page 78, Karen says, "I know that there are ways to control the world. I've been working on them for a while now. If I stomp my feet five times before the garage door closes, then nothing bad will happen to me. If I microwave a hot dog for eleven seconds at a time, hitting START over and over again until it is finally warm, then no more space shuttles will explode." Why does Karen feel this way? Have you ever felt this way, too?

12. What do you think of Karen's friendships with Samuel, Dina, and Jessica? How are they alike or different?

13. Can you relate to Karen's first sexual encounter with John Wise? Did you feel similar pressures in junior high or high school?

14. How is Karen's relationship with John Banks different? How is she "reborn through John," as she says on page 188?

15. How does the author use doll imagery throughout the book? And why?

16. Were you surprised by the end of Chapter 25? Did the author allude to this trauma at other points throughout the book? What do you think of the idea that the body remembers what the mind forgets?

17. On page 229, Karen talks about the power she finds with girls. Do you feel this way, too? Do you find strength in your female friendships?

18. How has Karen's mother's illness affected her? How has it affected the entire family?

19. Why do you think Karen needs to leave home? Can she rewrite the story of where she came from?

20. What do you think will happen to Karen's relationship with her mother in the future?

# Acknowledgments

Alice Martell: The superstitious little girl in me saw the signs, and hoped I wouldn't jinx things with my dream agent. Thank you for being smitten.

Lara Asher: Your enthusiasm and support guided me through all the tricky parts of publishing. Thank you for editing my work with such warmth and insight.

Paula McLain: Every girl needs a literary fairy godmother. Thank you for being mine.

The editors of Matter Press, the *Bellingham Review,* and Monkeybicycle, who graciously published small pieces from this book in earlier forms: Thank you for giving me an audience when I needed it most.

Conor Oberst and Laura Jane Grace, whose songs I listened to often while writing this book: Thank you, thank you.

Melissa Bisesi: You light the way for me, even through the darkest midnights of life. Thank you for your friendship, now and beyond.

The entire Dietrich family: You're clearly the best in-laws in history. Thank you for loving me as fiercely as your own. I'm especially grateful to Bob and Jill Dietrich for being on my team.

My sisters: Thank you for not looking away, even during the scary parts.

Robert: You came into my life and woke me up in every way. Thank you for that, and for everything else.

RJ: I'd have to invent new words to explain how much I love you. Thank you for dreaming of tiny houses with me.

# About the Author

**Karen Dietrich** worked as a restaurant hostess, a video store clerk, a credit card customer service rep, and a high school English teacher before earning an MFA in poetry from New England College in 2008. Her poems and essays have appeared in *Pittsburgh City Paper*, *Nerve*, the *Bellingham Review*, the *Pittsburgh Post-Gazette*, *PANK Magazine*, and elsewhere. She lives in Greensburg, Pennsylvania, with her husband and son.

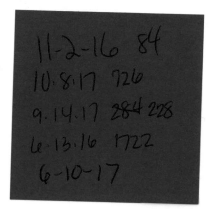